A COLLECTOR'S GUIDE TO

—

SWORDS,
DAGGERS &
CUTLASSES

—

A COLLECTOR'S GUIDE TO

—

SWORDS, DAGGERS & CUTLASSES

—

CHARTWELL
BOOKS, INC.

GERALD WELAND

A QUINTET BOOK

Published by Chartwell Books
A Division of Book Sales, Inc.
110 Enterprise Avenue
Secaucus, New Jersey 07094

This edition produced for sale in North America,
its territories and dependencies only.

ISBN 1-55521-726-5

This book was designed and produced by
Quintet Publishing Limited
6 Blundell Street
London N7 9BH

Creative Director: *Terry Jeavons*
Designers: *Wayne Blades, Stuart Walden*
Project Editors: *Sally Harper,*
Damian Thompson
Editor: *Lydia Darbyshire*
Photographer: *Martin Norris*

Typeset in Great Britain by
Central Southern Typesetters, Eastbourne
Manufactured in Hong Kong by
Regent Publishing Services Limited
Printed in Hong Kong by
Leefung-Asco Printers Limited

CONTENTS

INTRODUCTION

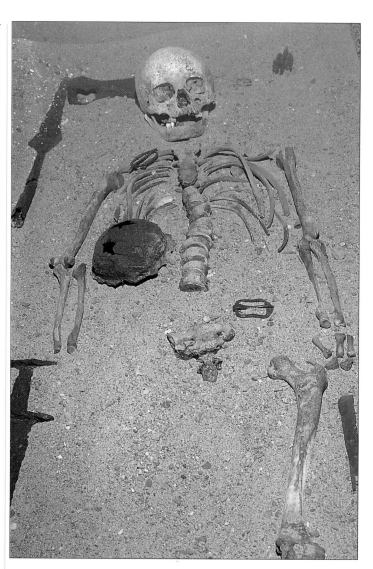

Edged weapons have been the primary tool of warfare for a hundred generations, and they are still the stuff of nightmares. Even today, when most killing in conflict is done impersonally, there is still something particularly horrifying about the thought of a covert reconnaissance unit inflicting silent death on unwary sentries.

An edged weapon may be defined as any implement designed for cutting and that possesses a blade more than twice as long as it is wide. Many weapons may be so defined, for over the years man has evolved an amazing number of ways to inflict death on his fellows. And in these days of modern warfare, when the slayer is rarely sufficiently close to the slain to see (let alone distinguish) him, edged weapons have become increasingly popular among collectors of militaria.

Part of the reason for this growth in interest lies, as it does with all collectables, in the desire to invest in objects that will appreciate in value. In this respect, some collectors regard militaria as others might regard fine porcelain or a painting, and there is no doubt that a rare or historical sword or knife will increase in value over the years. Other collectors admire edged weapons for the skill and artistry with which they were made and acquire, say, scimitars or Japanese daisho for their visual appeal.

However, few would dispute that the real attraction of edged weapons is that, unlike an Impressionist painting or a Royal Worcester teapot, a sword or a dagger or a knife allows the owner to 'touch' history. But it is not only that holding a sword that was used at the battle of Waterloo or an early 15th-century Italian dagger enables us to imagine that we are in contact with the people who wielded them. Weapons, in a way that a stamp, a painting or a piece of porcelain can never do, represent the journey of mankind through history.

This book attempts to trace that journey by discussing the major types of edged weapons in terms of history. There are four main chapters – covering swords, naval edged weapons, smaller blades and edged weapons from the Far East and India – and within each chapter are descriptions of the principle types of weapon as well as assess-

ments of the availability to collectors of each kind. The final chapter gives some practical advice to aspiring collectors about acquiring edged weapons as well as outlining some of the pitfalls.

Collecting is a never-ending process and one that rarely goes according to plan. When you purchase your first sword or dagger you are beginning an enthralling but frustrating search. You will probably never acquire everything you want – and you may end up with pieces that you did not, initially, imagine you would ever buy. But that is part of the excitement.

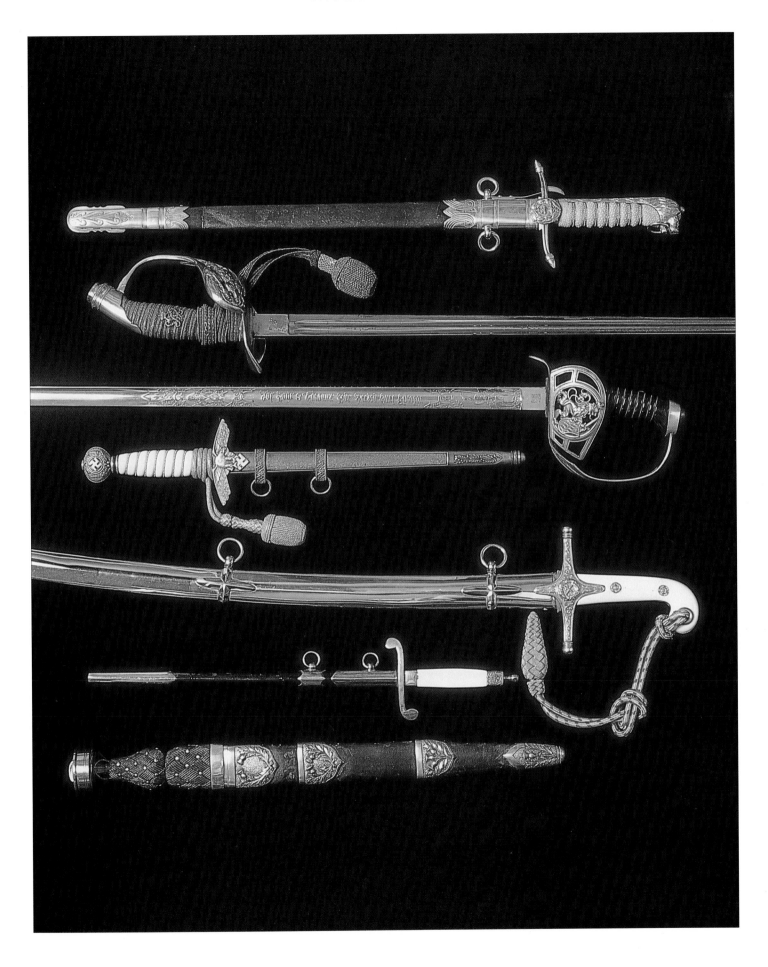

THE PARTS
OF A SWORD

The example below is specifically a naval cutlass, but for present purposes, this is not important.

The **HANDLE** (or mount) is in this case very plain. The knuckleguard and handguard are melded together to form one part, and the tang button at the top of the tubular hilt is negligible. There is but the slightest hint of a quillon.

The **SHOULDER**. Whether single- or double-edged, it was customary to leave several (up to six) inches of the cutting edge unsharpened. This was advisable in case the user's hand somehow slipped over the handguard. On such weapons as rapiers or basket-hilted broadswords the shoulder was frequently dispensed with.

The **EDGE** (or cutting edge), which was sharpened for use in battle. On almost all curved weapons, with the exception of some 18th-century backswords, the edge is that which curves backwards or upwards, depending on the perspective

The **BLADE**.

The **BACK EDGE** is the unsharpened edge on any single-edged weapon. Obviously a double-edged weapon would not have a back edge.

The **FALSE EDGE** was rarely seen (and almost never on a curved cutlass or sabre). However, on some longer single-edged swords it was customary to sharpen a few inches of the back edge as well. This made penetration and withdrawal of the blade that much easier when thrusting.

The **TIP**.

THE PARTS OF A HANDLE

Though 'handle' is the correct generic term for this part of the sword, as this is a detail of a British naval presentation sword it should, strictly speaking, be referred to as the 'mount'.

The **TANG BUTTON** is found on heavier or more elaborate swords, but not always – and rarely on knives. Adding stability and strength, it was inserted, like a screw, into the butt of the tang (inside the hilt).

The **KNUCKLEGUARD**.

The **RICASSO** is the small, flat or concave plate containing a slot through which the blade is passed. It served several functions, chiefly stability to the hilt and ornamentation. When combined with the crossguard it formed what is generally termed (vaguely) the handguard. Only better-made swords ever had a ricasso, though they were found in every part of the globe where edged weapons were taken seriously – at least in the past 1,000 years or so.

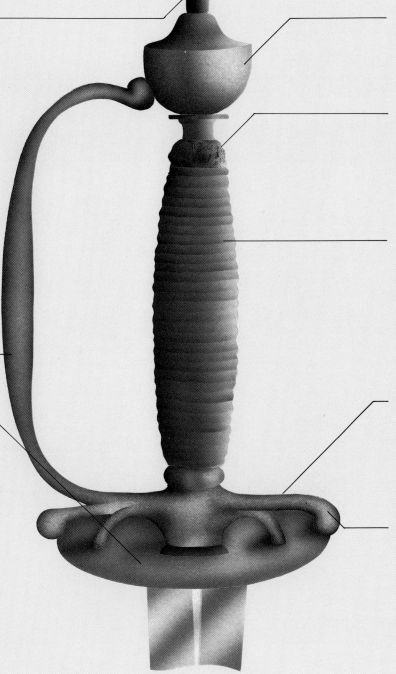

The **POMMEL**, which served to support the rear of the hand.

The **HILT** is that part of the weapon covering the tang, and that which was obviously used to hold the weapon.

The **GRIP** represents whatever covering was adhered to the hilt. Though closely allied to the hilt, it should not be confused as being the same thing: some hilts had no grips *per se*.

The **CROSSGUARD**. Designed to prevent slippage of the hand over the blade, this feature can be seen in the very earliest of weapons.

The **QUILLON**. In the case of rapiers, these frequently became so elaborate that they formed a basket hilt around the entire hand. Those shown here, by contrast, are very modest.

CHAPTER ONE

SWORDS

SWORDS

The development of metal-working techniques is thought to have begun in Mesopotamia in 3500–3000BC. Copper was one of the earliest metals to be used by man, and although today the principal deposits are in the US, Chile, Canada, Zambia and Zaire, long ago it was found in many parts of Europe and the Middle East. The early Minoans, c 2900BC, are known to have fashioned implements from gold, silver and copper. Also found were deposits of tin, and this was used, with copper, in the earliest alloy known to man – bronze. Copper had been used to make weapons, but the discovery of bronze and its suitability for casting meant that, for the first time in history, strong blades of real length were able to be fashioned.

Copper swords had, in effect, been nothing more than long daggers, but cast bronze blades of 75–90cm (30–36in) in length could be made from this fine-grained and malleable material, which, when prepared properly, had a high ten-

sile strength and offered considerable resistance to damage and corrosion. The shape of these early bronze swords also began to change, with a central rib being added to maintain maximum rigidity in thrusting.

During the third and second millennium BC migratory races, known today as People of the Sea, appeared in Europe. These people, who used metal, built impressive houses and traded with Crete and the islands of the Aegean, settled on most of the Greek mainland. It is clear that these people were not Greek, and they may have come from southern Russia.

These raiders made several innovations to the weaponry of the time. The type of warfare they pursued made a sword suitable for cutting as important as a thrusting weapon, and they developed a double-edged sword with a strong point, which could be used in both ways. Making weapons of this kind was difficult, however, because of the problems of attaching the tang (the

ABOVE:
A sword hilt of cast bronze with a green patina. The blade is missing, though the rivets for it remain. Danish, late Bronze Age (c 1200 BC).

PREVIOUS PAGE:
Swordfighting was quite common in the American Revolution. This picture commemorates an engagement between British forces under Colonel Banastre Tarleton and troops led by Francis 'Swamp Fox' Marion in 1780.

THE SONG OF ROLAND: AN ENDURING SWORD MYTH

Feudal history springs to life in the long, narrative poems known as *chansons de geste,* and one of the best known and one of the earliest was the *Chanson de Roland,* which was written in the 11th century and which is devoted almost exclusively to fighting and feudal intrigue. Roland, who died in 778, was a young French soldier, killed at Roncesvalles during Charlemagne's invasion of Spain. Roland was actually killed by the Basques, but in the *Chanson de Roland* the enemy has become the Saracens. The 4,000 lines of the *Chanson* relate how, when Charlemagne had been in Spain for six years, he sent Ganelon, Count of Mayence and one of Charlemagne's Paladins, as an ambassador to Marsillus, the pagan king of Saragossa. Inspired by jealousy, Ganelon betrayed to Marsillus the route the Christian army planned to take on its return to France. The pagan king arrived at Roncesvalles just as Roland was conducting through the pass a

rear-guard of 20,000 men. Roland fought until 100,000 Saracens were slain and only 50 of his own men survived, when another army of 50,000 poured into the pass. Roland blew his enchanted horn, and, although Charlemagne heard him, Gamelon persuaded him that Roland was hunting deer. Roland was left to his fate.

Roland's sword, Durandal (sometimes Durindana or Duranda), had, according to legend, belonged to Hector and, like the horn, Roland had won it from the giant Jutmundus. It had in its hilt a thread from the cloak of the Virgin Mary, a tooth of St Peter, one of St Denys's hairs and a drop of St Basil's blood. The *Chanson de Roland* relates how, after he had been mortally wounded, Roland strove to break Durandal on a rock to prevent it falling into the hands of the Saracens, but, because it was unbreakable, he hurled it into a poisoned stream, where it was destined to remain for ever.

part of the rear of the blade that runs through the handle) to the hilt. When swords were nothing more than long knives, it was a simple matter to insert the rear of the blade into the handle and to hold it firm with a few small rivets. Forward and backward thrusting movements caused little structural strain. But swords intended to be used in a number of ways were more complicated to construct. The problem was solved by making a special groove in the tang into which the shoulder (or rear) of the blade might fit snugly and tightly. Larger rivets held them together.

More efficient, of course, was to cast the blade and tang as a single piece, but this practice does not appear to have been widely followed, partly because it made it necessary to cover the handle with a material such as wood or bone to provide a decent grip in battle. The wood or bone would generally become dislodged after even only limited use and could render the weapon useless, even in the hands of an expert swordsman. In addition, the primitive construction methods made elaborate, one-piece weapons difficult to produce.

It would be wrong to believe that weaponry was standardized throughout Europe at this time and that construction techniques were uniform. Long before the rise of the nation states, tribes and groups of tribes struggled with each other for supremacy. It would appear that, even at this early stage, the techniques and designs of 'military technology' were closely guarded secrets.

The introduction of iron brought further changes to sword construction, for it was, of course, infinitely superior to bronze in many ways. Nevertheless, the two types of blade continued to co-exist for several centuries. The Hittites, who had evolved in Asia Minor c2000BC and by c1500BC had established a strong, centralized government with a capital at Hattusas (near to modern Ankara), appear to have been responsible for the great technological advance – the smelting of iron. However, they do not seem to have benefited from the discovery in the making of weapons. By 1200BC the Hittite kingdom was gone, and it was followed by the formation of empires that dominated the Near East. The first of these was established by the Assyrians, who came from northern Mesopotamia, on and to the east of the river Tigris, and who, by 665BC, controlled the area from the southern frontier of Egypt, through Palestine, Syria and much of Asia Minor, to the Persian Gulf in the southeast. The Assyrians are, in fact, often credited with having developed the sword as we know it today, and their success in extending the frontiers of their empire was, in part, due to their use of iron weapons, and because iron is more common than copper or tin, it was possible for them to arm more men more cheaply.

It was during the second millennium BC that sheaths first appeared, for when it was found that iron weapons could be sharpened to an edge previously unknown with bronze implements, it obviously became necessary to protect the blades when they were not in use. Initially, the benefits that accrued from sheathing swords were marginal, for the early examples tended to be made of wood or even bronze, and unsheathing and returning the blade to its resting place just a few times inflicted all kinds of damage. Leather sheaths became widespread c1000BC.

Major developments in the making of swords took place in 900–500BC, but even at this time they appear to have been regarded as much as art forms as weapons. Magnificent grips and in-tricate decoration seem to have been as important as effective blades. Because iron increased the tensile strength, blades were often more than a metre (40in) long, almost too long to be effectively wielded at a time when, archaeologists tell us, a man standing 1.7m (5ft 6in) tall was a robust specimen. By the time Rome was founded about 750BC all the so-called barbarian tribes of Europe were using these long swords, although battle axes and spears seem to have been the preferred weapons. It was not until c500BC that these swords came to be regarded as weapons for combat, and at this time most of the decoration vanished and the emphasis was on the functional characteristics of the blade. Swords from this period are usually all described as 'pre-Roman', although there were considerable regional differences in style.

One of our main sources of knowledge of weaponry dating from c500BC is the La Tene site in France, where iron weapons have been found. It is clear that by this time iron's supremacy over bronze for the making of weapons had been widely recognized. Bronze was still used for gilt ornamentation and sometimes handles, but had otherwise completely fallen from use. Swords had begun to decrease in length, to 75–90cm (30–36in), and something approaching mass-production appears to have been possible. At this stage, too, the first 'trademarks' seem to have been used to identify not only to which tribe a sword belonged but also where it was made.

There were still major problems, however, even with iron swords. Repeated impact in conflict frequently caused the handle to twist around the tang if improperly riveted, and this proved an almost insuperable difficulty, especially when the foe was the well-organized Roman legions with their gladii (see below). Eventually, of course, the Romans were defeated, and the long sword proved more effective, especially when it was used on horseback to cut, rather than thrust. As the Roman Empire began to give way in the 3rd century AD, the long sword gained supremacy, and it remained essentially unchanged throughout the early Middle Ages and until the period of Charlemagne.

In the early Middle Ages swords became, if not longer, at least bulkier. By this period grips were adorned with all manner of ornamentation, often being inlaid with precious metals or with pearl or other expensive materials. But because

SWORDS

RIGHT:
This excellent sixteenth-century portrait shows Edward VI, son of Henry VIII, who failed to live to his majority. Note the ear dagger, so popular with royalty at the time. Though the artist is unknown, the work is reminiscent of Hans Holbein, who painted so much of English court life in that period.

the sword was so large, if a blow was forcefully delivered, the sword was difficult to hold, and the combatant either dropped his weapon or, worse, his hand slipped down the unsharpened shoulder on to the blade itself. It was here that the quillon made its appearance. This was in essence a handguard between the grip and the shoulder of the blade. Originally, the quillon was a single, straight bar, and was often called the crossguard; later it became more elaborate, curving back towards the pommel on the rear of the grip and forming what was known as the counterguard. The quillon thus not only made it almost impossible to lose the grip on a weapon but also protected the hand from injury.

Throughout the early Middle Ages advances continued to be made in the design of swords, most improvements being made in the area now known as France. Grips became more defined and elaborate; the pommel at the rear began to show curves and gilded decoration; but blades continued to be used only for cutting or, more accurately, hacking. In folklore, literature, art and practice the preferred technique was to strike the opponent with an overpowering stroke. Contemporary references almost always allude to 'hewing' the foe with one masterful stroke.

In the days of chivalry and romance a knight's sword and horse were his two most highly prized possessions, and it was customary to give each a name. Among the most famous such swords are Balmung, one of the swords made by Wieland for Siegfried; Courtain, the short sword of Ogier the Dane; Tizona, the sword of El Cid; and, perhaps the most famous of all, Excalibur, the sword of King Arthur. In particular, the preoccupation with swords and swordsmanship revealed in the *chansons de geste* tells us much about the attitudes to chivalry and the knightly life prevailing in 11th- and 12th-century France.

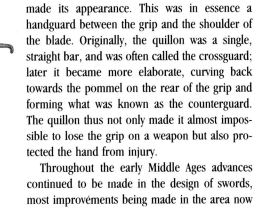

FACING PAGE:
This portrait of the Frenchman Gautier de Chatillon depicts the invasion of Egypt in 1249 during the Crusades. During this campaign King Louis IX (St Louis) was captured and reached the Holy Land only after paying the proverbial king's ransom.

RIGHT:
This extremely rare Italian medieval sword, with gilt pommel and crossguard, dates from c1400.

BELOW:
A number of interesting features adorn this Scottish military presentation sword, dating from 1807. Note the finely etched trophies, lion's head crest, the motto '*Semper Fidelis*' and the personal inscription.

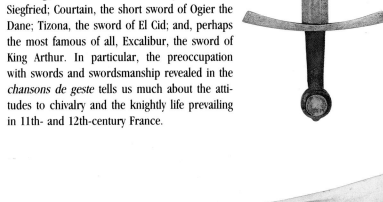

LEFT:
Dating from 1360, this rare medieval sword (of unknown origins) has a blade of 84 cm (33 in).

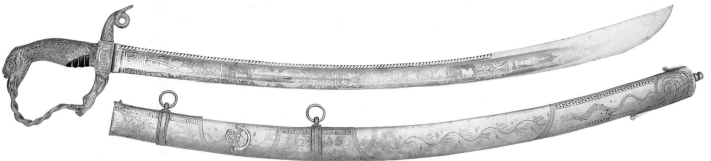

- Bellum ibi Gwido de Turri euasit -

The 13th and early 14th centuries are generally regarded as the zenith of sword craftsmanship, both in terms of function and beauty. Grips were engraved and inlaid; pommels were large and highly decorated; and the crossguards above the shoulder of the blade were often so large and sturdy that they made the sword look more like a cross than a weapon. Throughout southern and western Europe there was a preference for blades that were efficient thrusting weapons, although elsewhere cutting blades remained dominant. All this changed in the mid-14th century, however, after the Battle of Crécy (1346).

This early battle of the Hundred Years' War (1337–1453), in which Edward III of England defeated the forces of Philip VI of France, was a watershed in military history. The English longbowmen (who were, as it happens, shooting their arrows downhill) overcame the massed cavalry ranks of the French, and although medieval chroniclers are notoriously unreliable, it is reported that no fewer than 1,542 French noblemen and knights had perished together with some 20,000 others.

A scene from the Battle of Aljubarrota, Iberia, in 1385, showing men at arms duelling with two-handed swords. In this battle Portuguese ruler John I triumphed with English help. He thereby repulsed a Spanish invasion. It led to the Treaty of Windsor in May 1386 between England and Portugal, which is still in force to this day.

RIGHT:
A Model 1889 Bavarian cavalry officer's sword. These were in service right through the early days of World War I, though the Germans were one of the first to realize the deadly nature of the machine-gun and abandon cavalry warfare. The hinged guard allows it to lie flat. The lion emblem, whether facing, recumbent or rampant, was a popular motif for most European countries historically.

Armies suddenly became larger and more mobile, and, while it was difficult to find quantities of good longbowmen, contingents of able-bodied men who could wield a sword could quickly be found. Soon the use of swords had so proliferated that they were being issued *en masse* to infantry throughout the 15th and 16th centuries. These swords were invariably double edged, sturdy and sharply pointed, to make them effective jabbing instruments. Only after the sword-bearing infantry had been sent in to attack the enemy front line were the cavalry deployed to exploit the breaches in the line and, in theory, to rout the foe. In consequence, the sword that had been familiar to the knightly class for some thousand years became outmoded and useless.

It was now that the cavalry sword began to evolve. The blade was either long and slender or short and broad, depending on the type of arm-aments expected to be borne by the enemy. Soon a distinctive type of weapon appeared, the specialized sword known today as the sabre. Although firearms were, despite their slow rates of fire power and erratic accuracy, increasingly used by the mid-18th century, the sabre survived and remained in use until World War I.

LEFT:
Early 17th-century sword for cavalry use, bearing on its blade the marks of Wolfgang Stantler, a Munich bladesmith. The wide double-edged blade is unusual in a cavalry weapon.

THE AMERICAN CIVIL WAR

A myth has evolved that there was something special about the armaments used in the Civil War. It is true that advances in fire power, signalling and so on were made, but there was, in fact, little that qualified as new, and this is certainly so of the edged weapons that were used. The cavalry sabre used by the US dragoons in snatching the western US from Mexico in the 1840s was essentially the same weapon used during the Civil War and, two decades later, to chase Indians. In 1840 the War Department had adopted a noncommissioned officer's sword based on a French model of 1822. Although this was handsome and looked graceful, it was a cumbersome, poorly balanced weapon; even so, it not only saw service

in every war from the 1840s but was also in use as late as the 1930s.

Confederate weapons were made in so many places that it is impossible to catalogue all the manufacturers. Many were made by village blacksmiths, and the Confederate forces were faced with the joint problems of few and poor quality weapons. Many were imported, especially from the UK, where one of the major suppliers was the Mole Company of Birmingham.

Federal swords were designed for appearance as well as effectiveness. They were used to designate rank and, often, branch of service. Sword and sword belt were expected to be worn at all times when on duty, and when the soldier was on foot, the sword was to be suspended from a special hook attached to the belt.

General officers were issued with a straight sword with a gilt hilt, silver grip and brass or steel scabbard. Almost all other officers were to own a simpler sword based on the War Department's 1850 pattern. General Order 21 of August 1860 extended the wearing of swords to other personnel. Medical and pay departments were to wear a small sword and scabbard based on the pattern designated by the Surgeon-General's Office. Officers of volunteer cavalry regiments were to adopt the cavalry sabre and scabbard

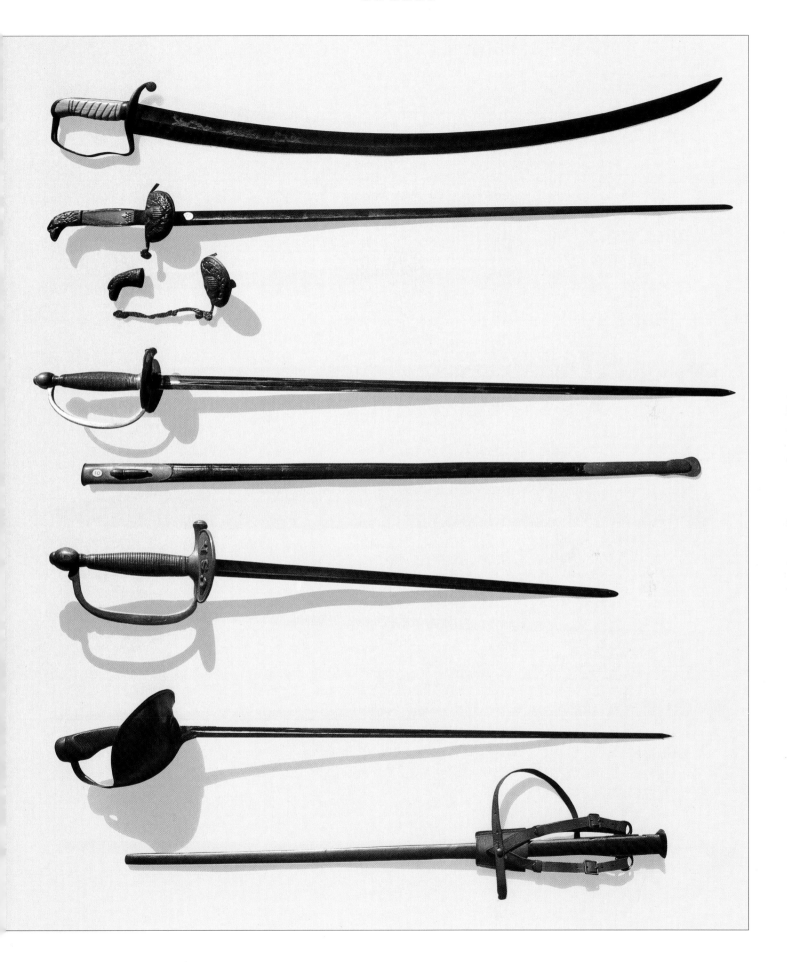

TOP TO BOTTOM:
A standard weapon manufactured between 1790 and 1810; based on the 1822-pattern British cavalry sabre, this weapon was made for a special force of dragoons, formed in March 1833; the Musician Sword, adopted by the US in 1840 to fulfil a support function in battle; standard French-style weapon, carried by US artillery from 1833 until c 1870; authorized for use in 1860, this variant on the standard officer's sword was useless for real battle, being too short and frail; sword issued to medical officers during the Civil War; this foot officer's sword was based on a French design and worn until 1872.

RIGHT:
General Philip Sheridan leading the successful charge of his cavalry at Cedar Creek during his Valley Campaign of 1864. Though 'Little Phil' barely got through West Point because of an assault on a superior cadet, he proved one of the most dashing, if cold-blooded, of American cavalrymen. It was he who later coined the immortal saying about the only good Indian being a dead Indian.

then in use. A sword based on the 1850 pattern was also ordered for all men of all ranks in the artillery and infantry, although few riflemen ever actually saw one. Other branches, such as the engineers, also had prescribed swords, and even the army musicians, who were expected to act as stretcher bearers on the battlefield, had swords.

According to the Ordnance Manual of 1861, 10 types of sword were officially in use, nine of which were approximately 1m (3ft) long, including the handle when scabbarded.

In reality, Federal officers wore swords of almost unlimited variety, and no great effort was ever made to enforce the regulations. However, field officers of all services who wanted a real weapon continued to use a version of the 1850 pattern sword. A light sabre, based, like the non-commissioned officers' sword, on a French pattern, was adopted for artillerymen in 1840, but it was not widely worn, although it was an attractive and useful weapon and remained in service for 50 years. Artillery officers wore swords like those of the enlisted men, but their weapons generally displayed modest decoration on the hilt or even on the shoulder of the blade.

The American General Lee taken Prisoner by Lieutenant Colonel Harcourt

LEFT:
The surrender of General Lee at Morristown, New Jersey, during the American Revolution, after Washington abandoned New York in 1776. The man accepting the sword is reputedly Colonel Banastre Tarleton.

The victorious charge of the US 2nd Dragoons at the Battle of Resaca de la Palma in May, 1846. This defeat repelled the Mexican invaders from Texas soil; never again would they occupy any part of 'American' terrain. The victory was the climax of the campaign which brought Zachary Taylor to the White House.

During the American Revolution British cavalry were regarded as elite units. This man is carrying the standard short musket and a routine version of the cavalry broadsword.

The most famous sword from this period is the cavalry sabre. This was, essentially, the Federal weapon first issued in 1840, and that had been based on a version of a French pattern first adopted in 1822. The American version was nicknamed 'old wristbreaker', which suggests its main shortcoming. In 1860 a lighter sabre with a narrower blade was introduced, although the two versions are difficult to distinguish at first glance. Many of the swords were purchased during the Civil War, with at least 11 firms contracted to supply the Federal cavalry. Most often seen these days are those made by J.T. Ames Co. of Chicopee, Massachusetts, and known as the Ames pattern.

As far as collecting Confederate swords is concerned, the weapons most often seen are the infantry officers' sword, the noncommissioned officers' sword and the cavalry sabre. Most of the infantry officers' swords will be the 1850 pattern (if its owner was a defector from the Federal Army) or a variant on it made by a southern blacksmith. Some will be imports from the Mole Company or another UK suppliers. The non-

1760

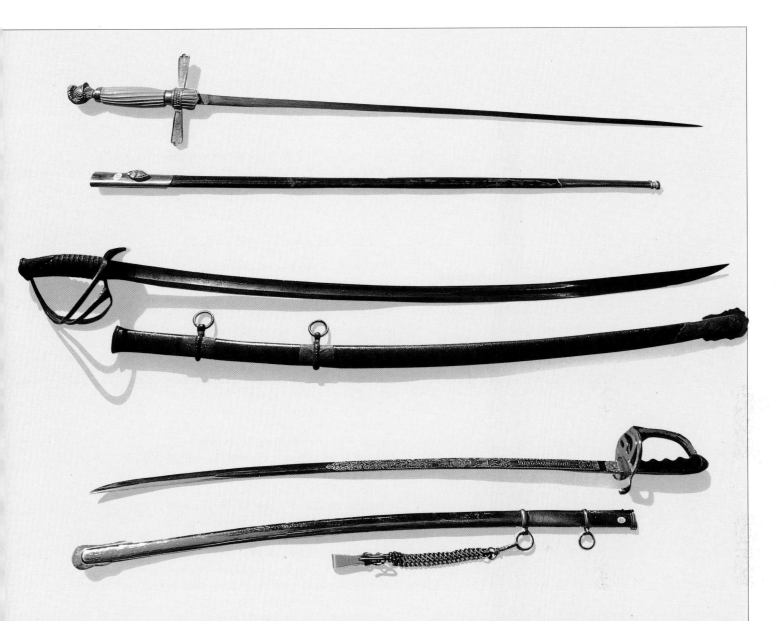

ABOVE TOP: This NCO sword was made during 1850–70 and was the standard weapon for US state militias at the outbreak of the Civil War. The US Volunteers were the primary levee of manpower for the Union army. **ABOVE MIDDLE:** A standard Confederate Infantry Officer sword. It may well be the easiest Confederate Civil war weapon to collect as it was made in substantial numbers.

commissioned officer swords and cavalry sabres are even less common, although they do appear at auction from time to time. It is sometimes difficult to identify them precisely, because the decoration on many of them is misleading or meaningless. In general, the number of Confederate weapons available to collectors is less than of Union weapons, partly because fewer were made and partly because they were less well made and therefore have not survived.

A collector is more likely to be able to build up a good collection of Union weapons. Staff and field officers' swords are not that difficult to find if you are persistent. Most will bear the date 1860, because of General Order 21, and most of these were probably worn by officers of the US Volunteers. The 1850 pattern is harder, though not impossible, to find.

Almost all the officers' swords from the Union seem to be available at present. It is even possible to find medical staff swords as well as some of the more interesting versions such as the pre-1850 light artillery sword that was based on the French pattern.

Many versions of the sabre are available, including the old Horseman's sabre, dating from the beginning of the 19th century. Other contractors who supplied weapons are the so-called Rose Contract of 1811 and the Starr Contract of 1812–18, and some of these may also have been used against the Indians and the British. A few may even have been carried by members of the US Volunteers. Versions of the 'old wristbreaker' can also be found, as can the lighter, 1860 version as well as some of the variants on it that were produced up to 1913.

ABOVE BOTTOM: In 1902 the US Army ordered a new officer sword based on the cavalry sabre. The blade was single-edged and slightly curved, usually no more than 76 cm (30 in) long and less than 2.5 cm (1 in) wide at the hilt. It remained the standard weapon as long as swords were worn in combat by the US Army.

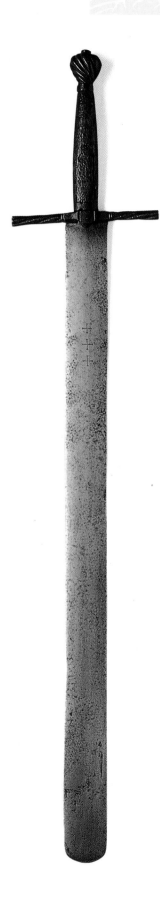

Let us start, however, by looking at some of the types of sword that are almost certainly beyond the reach of the average collector. This is not entirely perverse, for to exclude these swords would be to make the story incomplete, and they will, in any case, probably whet your appetite for what is to come.

BEARING SWORD

Bearing swords were never actually worn. They were made for ritual use at official ceremonies. The tradition is believed to have originated in the Byzantine Empire in the early 7th century. An arms bearer would carry an unsheathed sword, point upwards, in testimony to the power and prestige of the ruler behind whom he walked. Such swords generally had wide blades and were shaped as an isosceles triangle. They were covered in inscriptions indicating the purity and nobility of the ruler, and the hilts were normally bronze while the scabbards were traditionally covered in red velvet. Such swords can scarcely have been of much value as weapons.

Long after two-handed swords were deemed worthless in battle, they were still manufactured by specialist craftsmen for ceremonial purposes, and the assortment of bearing swords on display at festivals, tournaments of arms, royal weddings and funerals and so forth must have been dazzling if meaningless. Such swords were especially popular in southern Europe, although the phenomenon spread throughout the continent from the 11th century onwards.

The largest bearing sword in existence is in the Armoury of the Tower of London. It belonged to Edward, Prince of Wales (later King Edward V, one of the Princes in the Tower) and was made when he was created Duke of Chester in 1475. The sword has a German blade.

CORONATION SWORD

The most elaborate of all swords is undoubtedly the coronation sword. Such a weapon symbolized the authority of a monarch, and it had, of necessity, to be impressive. The most magnificent ever known is reputed to have been that worn by Charlemagne when he was crowned Holy Roman Emperor on Christmas Day 800 in St Peter's, Rome, by Pope Leo III. Charlemagne probably

also initiated the tradition of having the coronation sword blessed by the reigning pontiff.

Few coronation swords now exist. The most valuable and famous example is the sword used in the coronations of French monarchs since the 12th century, which is in the Louvre, Paris.

Coronation swords were functional only in that they were modelled on the weapons in use at the time. Their primary role was to represent the grandeur of the monarchy, and the goldsmiths, craftsmen and armourers who worked on them made them into works of art not weapons.

PAPAL SWORD

Then there are what have come to be known as papal swords. These are the long-bladed weapons used by pontiffs as a symbol of respect and admiration for the, primarily, military leaders whom they judged to be worthy of the title 'defender of the faith'. The custom began in the early 11th century and was followed assiduously for many centuries thereafter, the last such weapon being presented in 1823 by Pope Leo XII to the French Duke of Angoulême for capturing the Trocadero forts guarding Cadiz and so terminating a revolt against the Spanish king, Ferdinand VII. It was traditional for the swords to be blessed by the pope on Christmas Day, and for centuries it was rare for that day to pass without some ruler or military hero being so honoured.

Papal swords were usually presented to individuals. An exception was in 1511, when Pope Julius II awarded one to Switzerland in recognition of the loyalty and valour of the Swiss Guards, which still protect the pontiffs. This weapon may be seen in the Landesmuseum, Zurich.

Like bearing swords, papal swords had broad, double-edged blades, which were suitably impressive but otherwise useless. They were often heavily inscribed with religious exhortations. Such swords were always accompanied by a dome-shaped cap, on which was embroidered the figure of a dove, symbolizing the Holy Ghost. Like the swords, the caps were always blessed by the pontiff before being bestowed.

Because of their enormous intrinsic value, papal swords were often stolen, dismantled or melted down; a handful only are still extant, and most of these may be seen in Italy.

An incidental interest of papal swords is the history they reveal of papal involvement in European politics between the 10th and 19th centuries, for the recipients names have been recorded and allow the machinations and intricacies of papal politics to be traced.

PRESENTATION SWORD

Finally, there are presentation swords. These are closely related to bearing swords, but differ in that the recipient of a presentation sword will

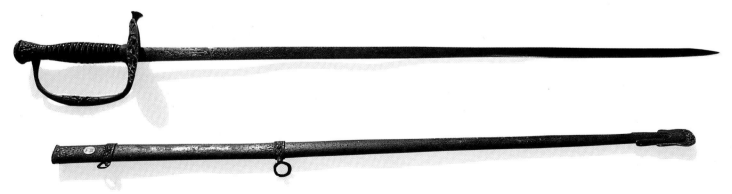

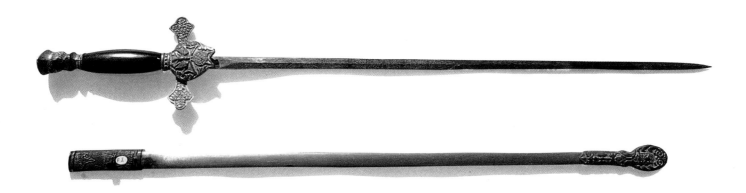

generally have earned it through efforts unrelated to an accident of birth or a successful marriage. These swords were symbols of honour bestowed on ranking members of the aristocracy and on other subjects of the realm who had earned recognition by way of either military prowess or political service.

The tradition is believed to have begun in Italy in the 10th century, when the sword presented was usually heavy. By the 18th century, especially in Britain, and later in the US, it was more usual for a light, dress sword to suffice. These swords were not, of course, intended to be used, even *in extremis;* instead, they symbolized the appreciation of a monarch or a nation for services rendered; they were gaudy rather than useful, with the finest swordmakers, jewellers and engravers employed to produce these works of art.

Several examples may be seen in museums around the world. The sword presented to the Marquis de Lafayette for his services in the American War of Independence is currently on display in the Castel Sant' Angelo, Rome, while among other European countries, Denmark maintains a considerable collection.

Russia once had the largest collection of presentation swords in the world. It was a long-established tradition for the tsars to award such swords to Cossacks as a reward for bravery.

Eventually, almost every officer in the Russian Army had received a similar sword, often with gold inlaid inscriptions and generally with gilt hilt and scabbard. In this way was born the 'golden weapon', whose possession was considered almost mandatory among the higher echelons of the Russian Army.

☆ ☆ ☆ ☆

It is, of course, highly unlikely that the average collector will ever obtain a coronation sword, a bearing sword or a papal sword. Presentation swords, however, are a different matter. They are frequently offered for sale at auctions and by reputable dealers. Among the most prized are Lloyd's swords dating from the early 19th century and American weapons of the same period that had been presented to men for outstanding service in the Union army during the Civil War (these are often known as GAR – Grand Army of the Republic – swords). Naval presentation swords are discussed on page 75.

ABOVE:
Edged weapons have been judged an excellent trophy or ceremonial object by many fraternal clubs and other brotherhoods throughout history. This stems from the large and popular Knights of Columbus organization in the United States.

BELOW:
Another example of a presentation weapon is the Masonic Sword.

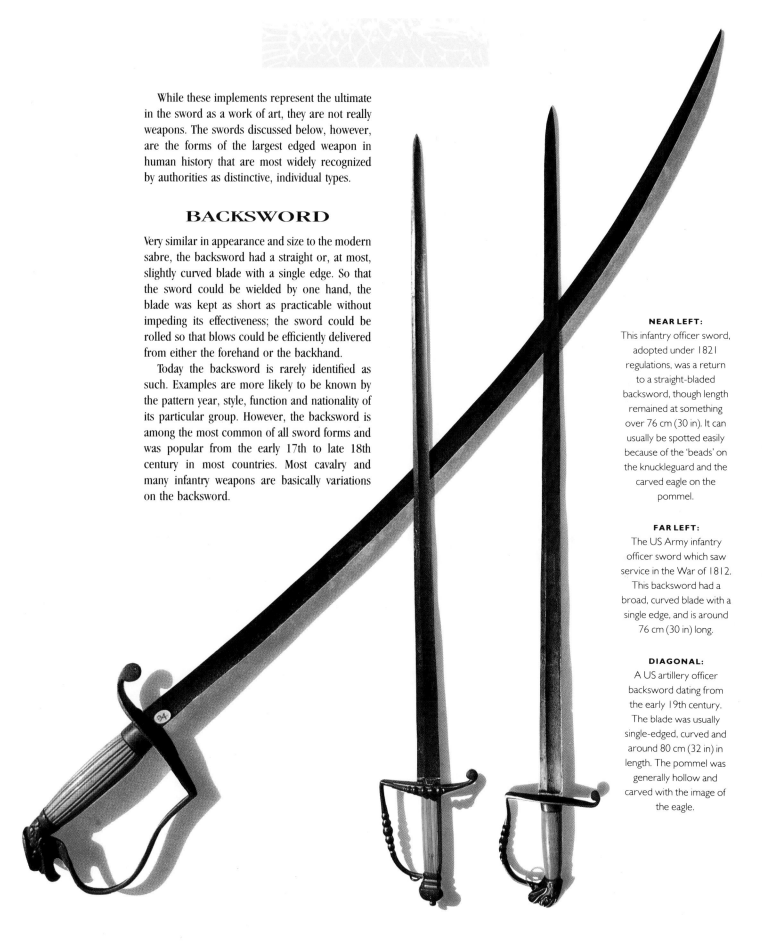

While these implements represent the ultimate in the sword as a work of art, they are not really weapons. The swords discussed below, however, are the forms of the largest edged weapon in human history that are most widely recognized by authorities as distinctive, individual types.

BACKSWORD

Very similar in appearance and size to the modern sabre, the backsword had a straight or, at most, slightly curved blade with a single edge. So that the sword could be wielded by one hand, the blade was kept as short as practicable without impeding its effectiveness; the sword could be rolled so that blows could be efficiently delivered from either the forehand or the backhand.

Today the backsword is rarely identified as such. Examples are more likely to be known by the pattern year, style, function and nationality of its particular group. However, the backsword is among the most common of all sword forms and was popular from the early 17th to late 18th century in most countries. Most cavalry and many infantry weapons are basically variations on the backsword.

NEAR LEFT:
This infantry officer sword, adopted under 1821 regulations, was a return to a straight-bladed backsword, though length remained at something over 76 cm (30 in). It can usually be spotted easily because of the 'beads' on the knuckleguard and the carved eagle on the pommel.

FAR LEFT:
The US Army infantry officer sword which saw service in the War of 1812. This backsword had a broad, curved blade with a single edge, and is around 76 cm (30 in) long.

DIAGONAL:
A US artillery officer backsword dating from the early 19th century. The blade was usually single-edged, curved and around 80 cm (32 in) in length. The pommel was generally hollow and carved with the image of the eagle.

BASTARD SWORD

This sword's name has caused the weapon itself to be misrepresented and misunderstood for centuries. In fact, the weapon is not especially exotic, having a long, straight blade, an elongated grip and a rounded pommel. It first appeared in the 15th century and was especially popular in southern Europe, although it was used in central Europe as well. The sobriquet derives from the fact that the sword could be used in a variety of ways, and it is generally better known among collectors as the hand-and-a-half sword. While it could be held and brandished effectively with one hand, the grip was sufficiently long and sturdy to allow it to be wielded by both hands in an overlapping grasp not dissimilar to that adopted when gripping a golf club. This allowed the combatant to increase the impact of any blow, and many people believe that this was, in some respects, among the most effective, and without doubt the most versatile, long-bladed weapon ever developed.

Bastard swords show up frequently at auctions and other sales. They are often identified merely as just another long sword and sold for their historic interest rather than any inherent generic value. Because of this, auction catalogue descriptions tend to be rather vague, and if you are anxious to add an example of this type of sword to your collection, take extra care when studying the catalogues.

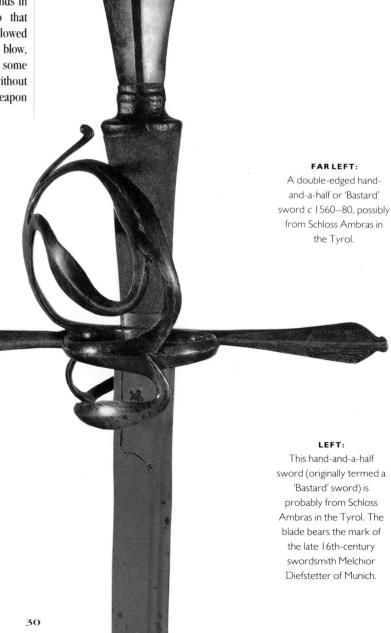

FAR LEFT:
A double-edged hand-and-a-half or 'Bastard' sword c 1560–80, possibly from Schloss Ambras in the Tyrol.

LEFT:
This hand-and-a-half sword (originally termed a 'Bastard' sword) is probably from Schloss Ambras in the Tyrol. The blade bears the mark of the late 16th-century swordsmith Melchior Diefstetter of Munich.

LEFT:
A Scottish clansman of the Highlands. Though the picture's date is uncertain, it is probably nineteenth century, since he is clearly wielding a basket-hilted broadsword (see overleaf), rather than the traditional Claymore.

BROADSWORD

The name broadsword is another term that causes confusion. Many broadswords are mistaken for the two-handed swords used in the Middle Ages (see below), but in fact, true broadswords bear no relationship to the type of weapon most of us imagine Macbeth wielded in defence of the realm he had usurped. The broadsword had a straight, wide, single-edged blade, and, by the 17th century, it was widely accepted as the standard military sword, becoming the weapon of the common soldier in place of the rapier, which had become the sword most often borne by civilians (see below). The broadsword usually had a basket-type hilt and, when owned by the wealthy or important, was often intricately decorated.

Broadswords can be found originating from all countries and from most periods: if a sword is from the English Civil War, the American War of Independence or a host of other conflicts, it is almost certainly either a backsword or a broadsword. Distinguishing the two, however, is a difficult task. Broadswords are generally a little sturdier and have larger handguards than backswords, but in general only experts will be able to identify the differences.

BELOW:
Late 18th-century Scottish basket-hilted broadsword (commonly – and wrongly – known as a 'claymore') with its original early 19th-century scabbard and belt for wear. This weapon was once owned by the Russian Prince Demidoff.

LEFT:
A standard broadsword carried by most US officers during the American Revolution. However, it was also popular with British officers and this one bears British regimental markings. The blade was generally around 63–69 cm (25–27 in) long, and animal head pommels were customary.

LEFT:
This basket-hilted broadsword dates from before the American Revolution. It was long the standard type for British mounted troops, but American cavalry also adopted it.

CLAYMORE

Today we are more likely to think of a landmine than a sword when we hear the word claymore, but in fact, the claymore was the two-handed sword of ancient Scotland, and its name derives from the Gaelic *claidheamh mór,* which means great sword. Although it became widespread only in the 15th and 16th centuries, its forerunner existed for several centuries before then. The sword had a long, heavy blade, a straight grip and a relatively small pommel. Several large quillons were always present to prevent the user's hands slipping down beyond the shoulder, and these were essential as claymores were usually employed with tremendous force to deliver an overhead smash. Only rarely were claymores ornamented – they were designed to be effective on the battlefield.

Claymores are frequently confused with a type of Venetian weapon known as the schiavona, a name originating from the word *schiavoni* (hired soldier). From the 17th century, Scottish weapons tended to be based on the Italian sword, although there is, in reality, little resemblance between the two and the newer versions were never as efficient in their purpose as the original claymore.

Claymores are extremely rare and are only likely to be found in a rare sale of an aristocratic collection by one of the major auction houses. Nevertheless, it is not impossible for a determined collector to find an example if he or she is prepared to search hard enough.

EPEE

Today épées are probably best known as one of the blades used in fencing. However, that incarnation is a comparatively recent development. Originally the épée was a stiff, heavy weapon with a blade that weighed 750g (27oz) or more. This may sound negligible, yet, combined with the shape of the blade, which, in cross-section, was triangular, and its length, 1.09–1.14m (43–45in), the épée was an impressive-looking weapon. Epées are excellent for parrying and thrusting, and they are generally the swords that we see in so many adventure movies. In fact, in real battles they were not terribly useful as it was almost impossible to inflict a serious wound on an opponent except by striking a vital spot with a thrust, and in the heat of battle the chances of achieving that were remote. Like the rapier, the épée eventually became nothing more than an essentially ornamental blade.

The sword was used to establish the modern sport of fencing. The movements for its proper employment were first described by the Italian swordmaster Achille Marozzo in his book *Il Duello,* which was originally published in Bologna in 1517.

The German version of the épée, the schlager, dates from the middle of the 16th century. Schlagers were more dangerous weapons, and had heavier blades, which were used for cutting.

Epées are not difficult weapons to collect (it sometimes seems that the world is awash with them), but the more highly prized examples – schlagers made in Heidelberg, weapons used in Olympic competitions or those with historic connections, for instance – are less easy to find and, in consequence, are often extremely expensive.

GLADIUS

It is almost impossible today for us to grasp the enduring power and grandeur of the Roman Empire. Rome was founded, according to tradition, in 753 BC, and the last emperor was deposed in AD 476. At the height of its sway, in AD 117, the empire covered all the lands of the Mediterranean littoral, extended into Mesopotamia as far as the Persian Gulf, spread north across Asia Minor to the northern shores of the Black Sea and encompassed all of western Europe, including what is now England, Belgium and Holland.

Throughout the expansion of the empire, the gladius was the standard infantry weapon of the Roman legions. (The word gladiator obviously derives from it, but in the arena only a small percentage in fact perished by means of the sword.) Few examples of the gladius have survived, but those that are extant give little indication that this must have been one of the most efficient weapons, let alone swords, of all time. The gladius was a short, stabbing sword. It had a double edge and a sharp, strong point. The blade was wide but originally rarely exceeded 60cm (24in) in length; in the latter days of the empire, in response to the needs of the cavalry for an effective cutting weapon, the blade was lengthened to 75cm (30in). The grip was remarkably uncomplicated – there was virtually no handguard, although a rounded pommel afforded an easy grasp in battle.

The strength of the gladius lay less in its individual construction than in how it functioned in conjunction with the legions' other equipment and the tactics adopted by the Romans. The sword was the natural ally of the scutum (shield), a slightly concave, rectangular object, approximately 1.2m (4ft) high and 75cm (2ft 6in) wide, made of a wooden framework covered with leather and, often, metal plates. In battle, the typical Roman tactic was to launch a fusillade of pila (javelins) and to follow this up with a charge

BELOW:
On this Roman tombstone found at Gloucester, UK, a Roman cavalryman is shown defeating the enemy, who wields a gladius. (Tombstone held by Gloucester City Museum, UK.)

LEFT:
Silver-mounted Turkish
sabre c 1800.

of legionaries brandishing their gladii – tactics not dissimilar to following up an artillery barrage with a bayonet charge. A legion's basic tactical component was the maniple, a subdivision of between 60 and 120 men standing three lines deep. By maintaining the correct spacing and discipline and by properly wielding their shields, the legionaries were well protected except against attack from the flanks or the rear. Against an enemy generally armed with smaller and, often, rounded bucklers, the gladius could be used to great effect to uppercut into the foe's torso.

The gladius was not really supplanted until nearly the end of the empire. By that time, the long swords of the Goths and other barbarian hordes had become pre-eminent, and the legions were no longer truly Roman in anything but name.

Most military historians and almost all true collectors would give almost anything to possess a Roman gladius; alas, gladii exist in only limited numbers and those are in museums. As a sword, the gladius is perhaps the single most important type in human history, embodying artistic, historic and geopolitical factors in a way that no other weapon has ever done. It is also just about the most impossible sword to collect.

KATZBALGER

This, the standard broadsword, came into widespread use in Germany and central Europe at the beginning of the 15th century, and it continued to dominate the battlefield for centuries thereafter. The oldest authentic example currently on display dates from 1515 and may be seen in Vienna, Austria.

The blade was broad, straight and double edged; the grip was heavy and the pommel wide, often flaring to afford an excellent grip. The sword was traditionally carried in a shoulder sling and borne, more or less parallel to the ground, with the point projecting rearwards and slightly upwards.

The name katzbalger may derive from the original sheaths, which were made of cat fur (*Katzenfell*) or, more probably, from the German slang word *Katzbalger*, which means an undisciplined tussle at close quarters. If this is the case, the name is somewhat misleading, for the sword's size meant that its user required a good deal of room for manoeuvre. Katzbalgers are sometimes, especially in parts of Europe, also known as landesknecht swords.

Katzbalgers can be found by collectors, but success is more likely through a European auction house, where it will probably be identified as a landesknecht sword. There are several versions of the standard katzbalger, and the type selected will, of course, depend on personal taste. Needless to say, as with all such historic swords, katzbalgers are not cheap.

KILIJ

Anyone who has seen a movie about the Middle East will probably be familiar with the shape of a kilij, although the name may have escaped them. In essence, a kilij is a Turkish sabre, and the sword dates from the rise of the Seljuk Turks, who, in 1055, established an empire in Asia Minor. Seljuk cavalry soldiers eventually brought about the downfall of the Byzantine Empire, but even in the mid-11th century they were unrivalled at warfare on horse.

The kilij's blade is quite different from blades seen elsewhere in the Moslem world. It was broader, shorter and less curved and could, therefore, theoretically be used for thrusting, although it seems to have been ineffective when used in that way. The kilij was almost wholly used as a cutting blade. The hilt, which resembled a pistol grip, was made of horn, ivory or even of semi-precious stone, and only a slim crossbar protected the hand. The kilij was never anything but a combat weapon, and any inscriptions are of a suitably warlike nature. Because of its modest curve, the scabbard was hung in front to allow the sword to be unsheathed quickly. Although it is the earliest Turkish weapon to be identified, it was so effective that its design remained unchanged and the blade length did not vary from 63–71cm (25–28in).

Kilijs are still made in some areas of Turkey, and a visit to the area might even yield an old example, as weapons that have been passed down from generation to generation over centuries are not impossible to find. Price and availability are, of course, difficult to predict, but kilijs are to be found, although obviously, the area itself or dealers with contacts there would be the ideal places to begin.

BELOW: Spanish cup-hilt rapier with a Toledo blade, late 17th century. This type of hilt offered heavy protection for the hand.

RAPIER

Although always more ornamental than useful, in the hands of an expert the rapier could be deadly. At the time that the broadsword (see above) became the standard military weapon throughout Europe, the rapier was developing into the customary sword for civilians of social standing.

Rapiers were essentially thrusting weapons. The handguards could be either elaborate or simple, but were more often the former. Although the rapier is identified most frequently with Britain, it seems to have appeared first in Spain and to have spread to the British Isles only in the 16th century. Nevertheless, it was in England that rapiers achieved their greatest popularity as social accoutrements; indeed, in 1571 an edict ordered the tips to be broken off rapiers exceeding a specified length and carried by courtiers entering Elizabeth I's court.

At first, rapiers were deemed suitable for use only as offensive weapons, although contemporary accounts suggest that they were effective against nothing more hazardous than the odd highwayman or recalcitrant merchant. It was recommended that a small shield be carried in conjunction with the rapier, although this advice does not appear to have been widely followed – possibly because to have done so would have appeared socially inept. It was, in any case, discovered that, wielded properly and using both its slashing blade and thrusting point, a rapier could inflict serious damage. Such a long and flimsy blade made its mastery rare. The rapier seems to have fallen from use even before it achieved the zenith of its popularity, although no film set in the 16th century is complete without its quota of actors wielding one. In the 17th century longer and heavier blades evolved, and the rapier was replaced by the smallsword (see below), a more functional weapon.

Acquiring rapiers is not impossible; indeed, they seem to be among the most often found weapons of recent centuries. They are also the most lavishly decorated, especially on the cross-guard and quillons, and for that reason they are popular with collectors. Potential collectors should, however, bear in mind that, for some reason, rapiers seem to be a regular target of thieves, and there are few major collectors who have not experienced problems of this kind.

FAR LEFT:
A French gentleman's rapier (c 1635–40), a very light weapon that would not hold its own when used against a sturdier blade.

NEAR LEFT:
A gentleman's rapier (c 1640–50), probably German. The blade is a German imitation of a Spanish style, and measures 100 cm (39.5 in).

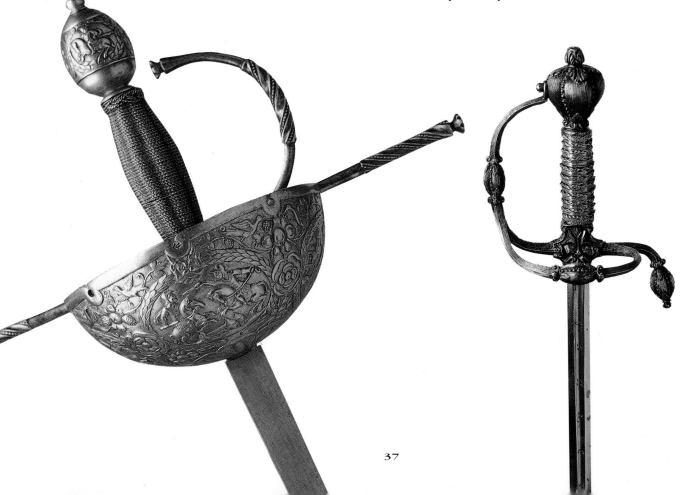

SABRE

Ask 100 people to draw a rough diagram of a sword, and it is probable that 98 of them would draw a sword bearing a remarkable resemblance to a sabre. The word is used to describe a type of sword with a single edge and a slightly curved blade. The sabre was the customary weapon of almost every country's cavalry throughout the 18th and 19th centuries. It was intended mainly as a cutting tool and was especially effective when wielded by cavalrymen, when it could inflict serious injuries to the heads and necks of the enemy's ground troops. In its gallant charge against the Russians, the Light Brigade under Lord Cardigan proved the sword's effectiveness at Balaclava in 1854 and would have enjoyed success if the timing had been better. Sabres could also be used by dismounted riders for thrusting, when it would effectively skewer opponents; unfortunately, because of the blade's curve, it was more difficult to extricate the sword from the foe's body.

The sabre is probably the easiest of the major swords to collect. The standard armament of cavalrymen for several hundred years, they continued to be made until comparatively recently, and no large collection does not contain between a dozen and a hundred examples. They are comparatively inexpensive, with prices ranging from several hundred to a few thousand pounds, and one of the main problems may be in selecting worthwhile swords. However, a collection of sabres would, to most enthusiasts of edged weapons, be among the most attractive of all groups of weaponry.

LEFT AND BELOW:
This chiselled and gilt sabre was possibly made for Henri II of France (c 1550) by the Italian swordsmith Daniel Serravalo of Milan.

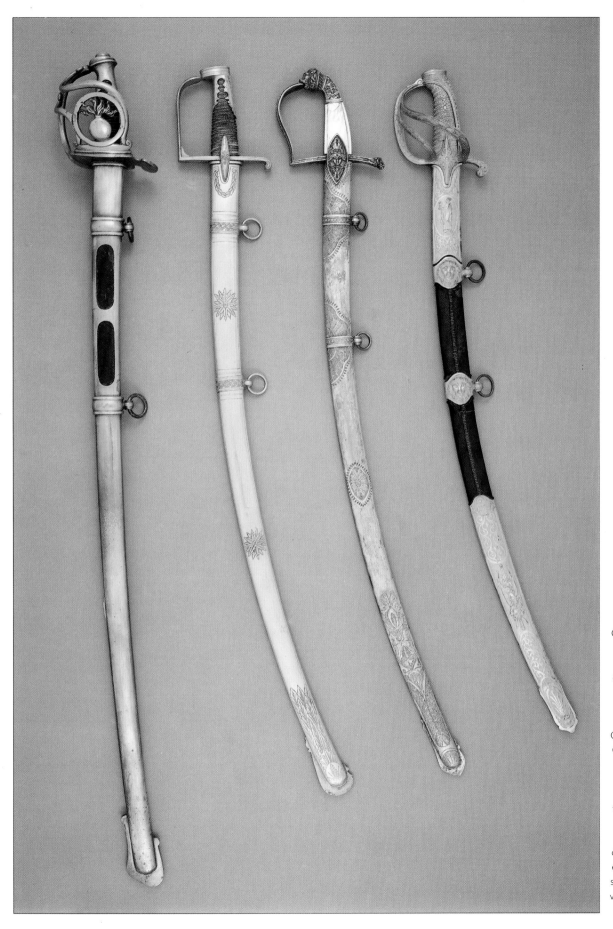

Craftsmanship and fighting efficiency combine in this selection of early 19th-century European sabres. **LEFT TO RIGHT:** A rare example for a trooper of the Mounted Grenadiers of the Imperial Guard, *c*1800; a sabre for a senior officer, possibly Imperial Guard, *c*1805; note the unusual grip, fashioned with mother of pearl scales, on this field officer's sabre, *c*1800; dated 1820, this example, encased in a black leather scabbard with gilt mounts, would have been worn by a senior officer.

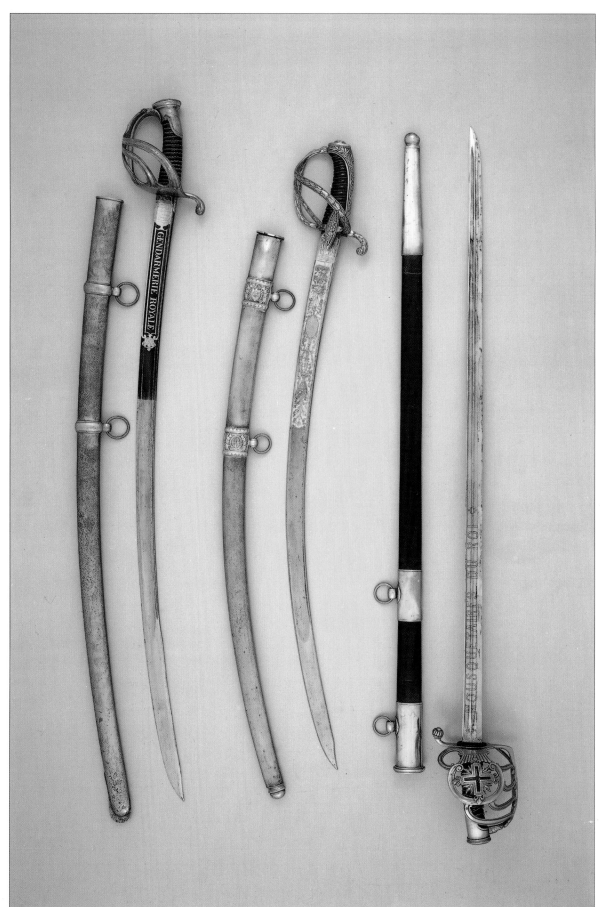

These French sabres are less rococo and more workmanlike than many contemporary examples.
LEFT TO RIGHT: A model 1817 sabre for an officer of Light Cavalry, Gendarmerie Royal; sabre for a superior officer of Lancers of the Royal Guard, c1815; a model 1814 sword for a trooper of the 1st Company of Royal Musketeers.

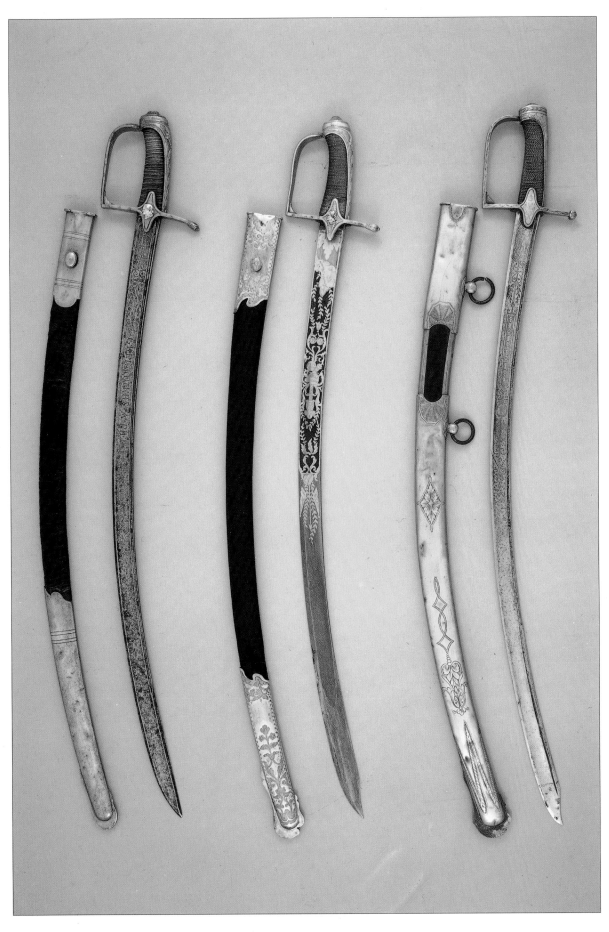

These three extremely rare senior officers' sabres represent the upper crust of military collectibles, and could fetch anything from £5,000–£8,000 ($10,000–$16,000) at auction. The regiments with which they are associated are as follows:
LEFT TO RIGHT:
Chasseurs à Cheval of the Imperial Guard, c1810; Infantry of the Imperial Guard, c1810; Foot Grenadiers of the Imperial Guard, c1805.

NEAR RIGHT:
The Confederate cavalry are judged by most military historians to have been the most effective component of their armed forces, and this is the type of sabre they employed. A popular article with collectors. **FAR RIGHT:** This single-edged sabre was issued for US cavalry officers in 1872. However, it had many defects as a combat weapon and was replaced by the 1902 pattern sword.

NEAR RIGHT: A variant of the famous British 1796 pattern cavalry sabre of the type used at Waterloo.
MIDDLE RIGHT: The Virginian Manufactory horseman's sabre was the first of its kind, and was popular between 1803 and 1820. **FAR RIGHT:** Dubbed 'Old Wristbreaker' when it supplanted the 1833 sabre, the heavy dragoon sabre of 1840 was too bulky and too long at 88.5–90 cm (35–36 in) to be wielded efficiently.

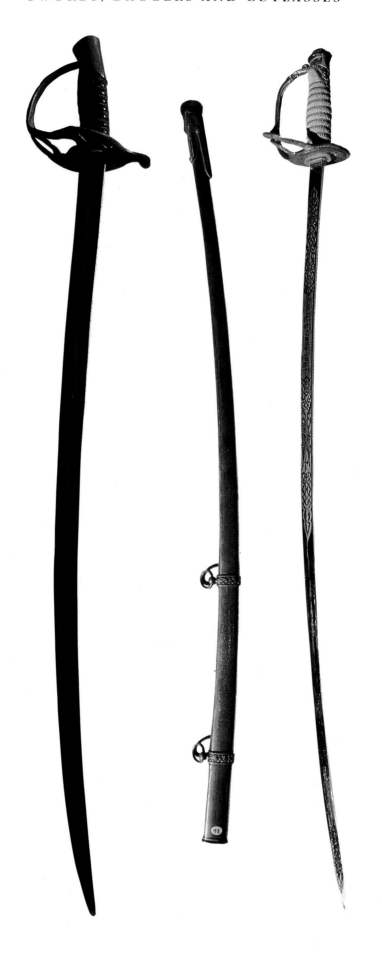

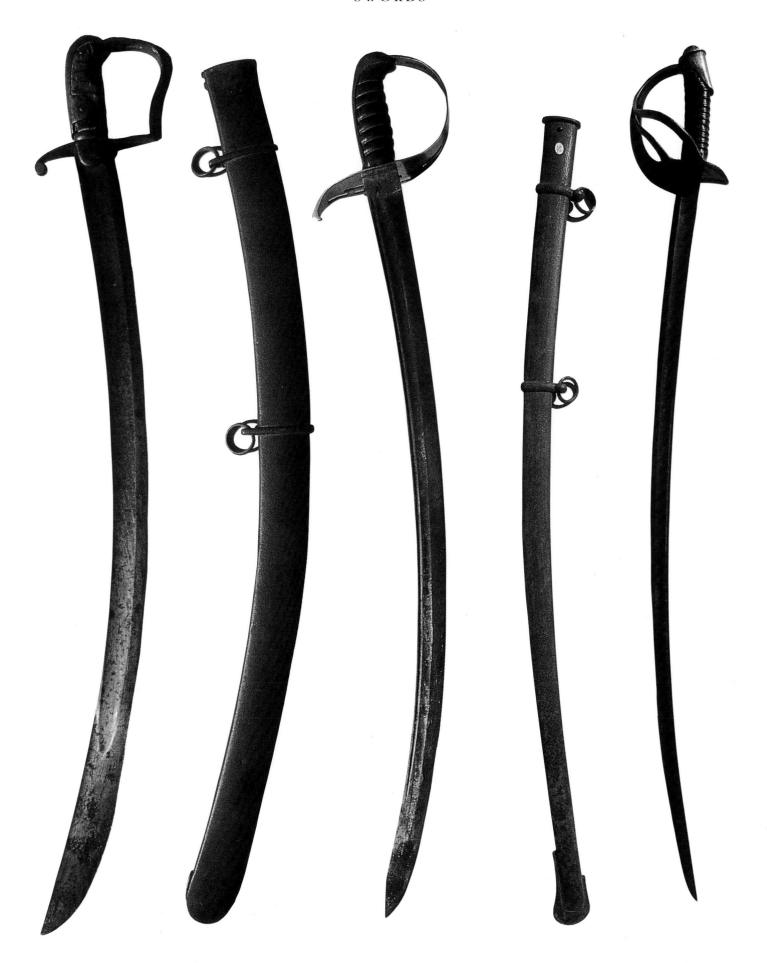

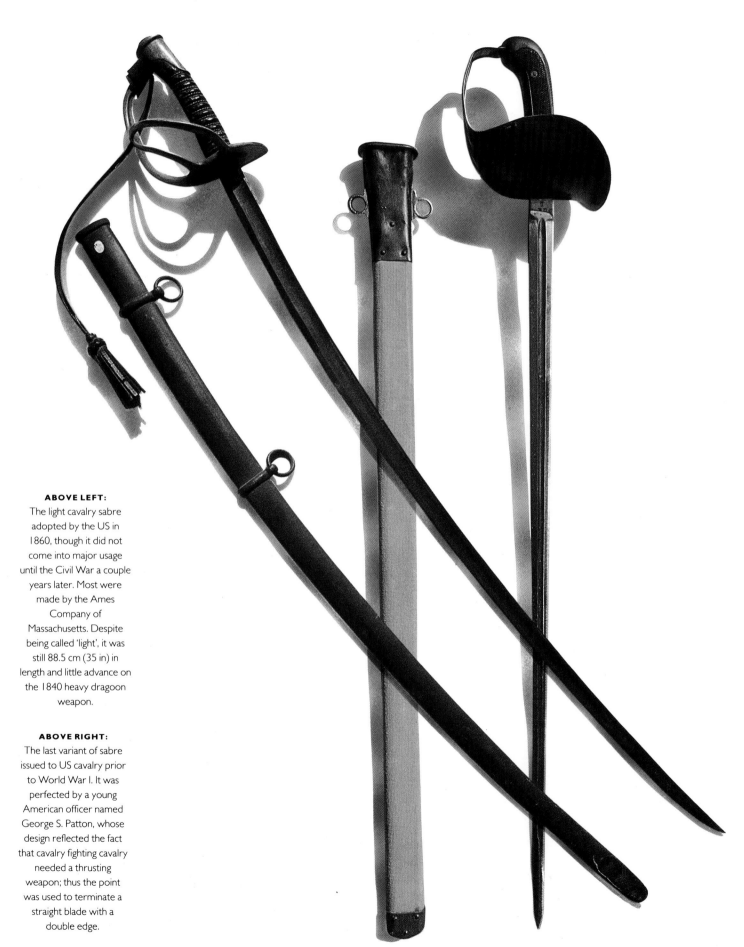

ABOVE LEFT:
The light cavalry sabre adopted by the US in 1860, though it did not come into major usage until the Civil War a couple years later. Most were made by the Ames Company of Massachusetts. Despite being called 'light', it was still 88.5 cm (35 in) in length and little advance on the 1840 heavy dragoon weapon.

ABOVE RIGHT:
The last variant of sabre issued to US cavalry prior to World War I. It was perfected by a young American officer named George S. Patton, whose design reflected the fact that cavalry fighting cavalry needed a thrusting weapon; thus the point was used to terminate a straight blade with a double edge.

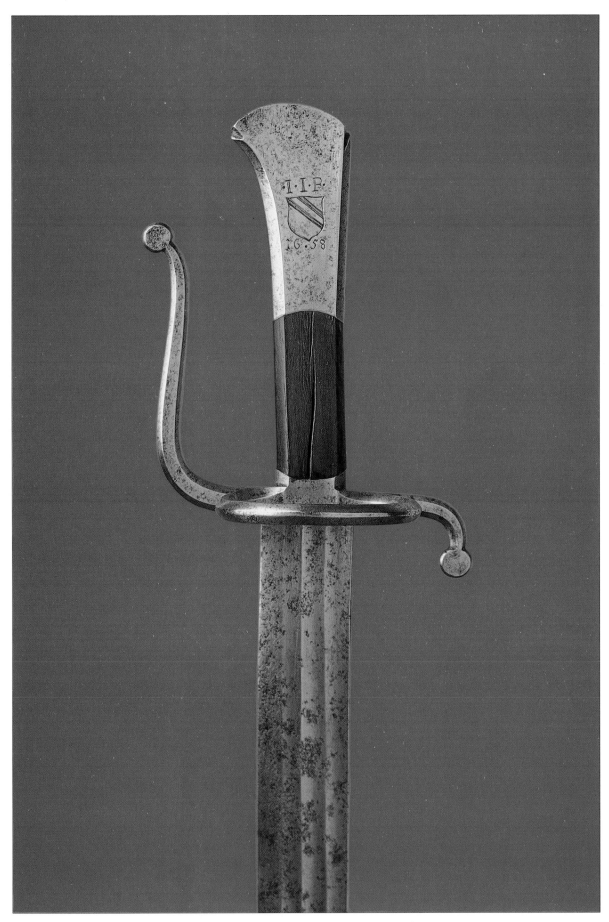

LEFT:
Hunting sabre bearing the owner's initials and the date 1658; German, made in the archaic 'Old Franconian' style which was fashionable at the time. Its blade is 76.8 cm (30.25 in) long and single-edged.

SCIMITAR

The word scimitar is often thought to be synonymous with Islamic hordes bearing down on hapless Christian pilgrims. In reality, however, the weapon was originally a hunting sword and was neither Turkish nor Arabic in provenance. The weapon known today as the scimitar was actually the shamshir, and the word scimitar appears to be a corruption of that name, which may mean lion's tail although the derivation is not certain.

Over the years the scimitar evolved into the sabre borne by the Persian cavalry. It had the pistol-style grip common to Islamic weapons, but, because of the extreme curvature of the narrow blade, the weapon was effective only for cutting as it was impossible to deliver a thrusting blow. Although the curvature of the blade was pronounced, however, it was always even and uniform, and the scimitar was, for that reason, extremely easy and quick to remove from its special scabbard. (The scimitar scabbard usually had a spring to make it snap open and facilitate drawing the weapon.) The sword was almost always carried, edge side down, hung from a sling on the left side of the rider.

The scimitar was the ultimate example of utility in warfare. It was never seen as anything but a weapon and rarely displayed any form of decoration or gilding. The only inscriptions found are, usually, the date of manufacture and, occasionally, the name of the owner. Despite its lack of ornament, however, or perhaps because of it, many authorities regard the scimitar as the finest and most beautifully proportioned sword ever manufactured.

It is not impossible to acquire scimitars, although whether the blade is an antique one or a recent example will be difficult to determine. Antique blades may be harder to locate, although scimitars were used over a wide area. Collectors should beware: a genuine scimitar will be very simple in appearance; heavily decorated and exotic-looking swords should be avoided.

LEFT:
Indian scimitar, the hilt and mounts of enamelled silver depicting fishes (the symbol of the reigning house of Lucknow); late 18th century.

LEFT:
Miniature Indian scimitar
mounted with enamel on
gold, late 18th century.

RIGHT:
Indian late 18th-century scimitar with a richly enamelled silver hilt, and a fine Persian blade dating from the 17th century.

SMALLSWORD

The smallsword was, in essence, a direct descendant of the rapier (see above). They were first seen at the end of the 17th century, when they were very simple in appearance, and they continued to be the standard sword for civilians for as long as edged weapons were carried. Viewed in cross-section, the blade was usually triangular, and it was designed solely for thrusting.

It shared another characteristic with the rapier: its light construction and the difficulty in using it properly made the smallsword one of the least hazardous weapons ever used. It appears that, no matter how enthusiastically wielded in a fight, the smallsword inflicted permanent injury on few people. Like any weapon, of course, in the hands of a determined man, the smallsword could be dangerous.

Smallswords are available to today's collectors. It is often difficult to tell precisely from descriptions in auction house catalogues, but it is likely that the majority of the long-bladed weapons offered for sale are some version of the smallsword as designed for civilian use. An enthusiastic collector could probably amass a good sized collection of these swords over a number of years, although some collectors regard them as among the least desirable of swords, partly because they have no military history and partly because they lack the physical charm and allure of, say, a rapier.

BELOW:
This smallsword, with a hilt of silver-gilt, was made by William Kinman about 1765–70, and retailed by Thomas Dealtry (a London cutler) whose name is engraved on the locket of the scabbard. Like most smallswords, its triangular blade bears some resemblance to a modern bayonet.

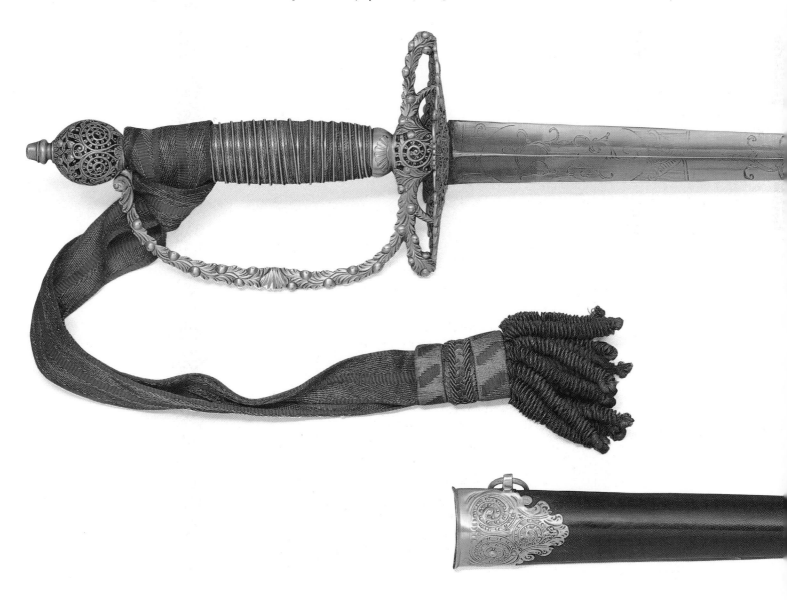

BELOW:
For centuries the Spanish Navy and Army both favoured a type of smallsword which was referred to by the name 'broadsword'. This one stems from c 1700.

RIGHT:
French smallsword; the hilt (of chiselled and gilt steel) was made in Paris, probably 1780–90. It was intended as a court sword or for ceremonial use.

BELOW:
The 1830 pattern smallsword used by French artillerymen. Considerable American weaponry was based on French examples throughout the 19th century.

TWO-HANDED SWORD

Most people think of the medieval broadsword when they hear the expression 'two-handed sword'; this is, in fact, a misapprehension, for the expression actually refers to any weapon large or heavy enough to require the use of both hands to wield effectively. These swords were usually used to direct overhead blows, but, such was their bulk, it was almost impossible to strike any but the least nimble of assailants.

The Swiss used two-handed swords almost exclusively until the end of the 15th century, when it was officially suppressed, and pikes became the customary weapon. Interestingly, it was only at this time that the Swiss earned their reputation as the best mercenary soldiers in Europe. In the 16th century the sword became the preferred method of execution throughout most of Europe, being used from the reign of Henry VIII. That monarch had to invite a French swordsman to England to dispatch Anne Boleyn in 1536.

Two-handed swords were most widely used in the East. Although neither the Chinese nor the Mongol hordes ever adopted the weapon, the Japanese katana (fighting sword) is among the best known swords of the kind.

It would be something of a challenge for a collector to find many two-handed swords – most are in museums – but some do turn up in auctions in Europe, although the catalogue descriptions are often too vague to allow certain identification to be made from the catalogue alone.

ABOVE:
A two-handed sword (or 'tuck') from Germany, early 16th century. A light weapon with a blade of 104 cm (41 in).

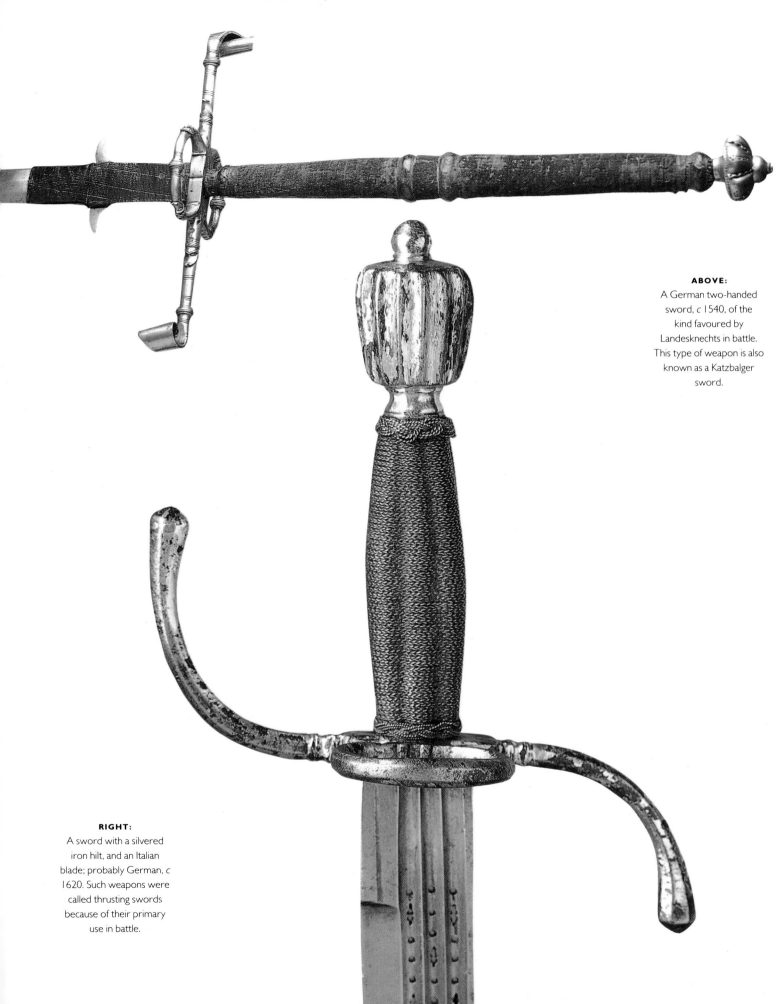

ABOVE:
A German two-handed sword, *c* 1540, of the kind favoured by Landesknechts in battle. This type of weapon is also known as a Katzbalger sword.

RIGHT:
A sword with a silvered iron hilt, and an Italian blade; probably German, *c* 1620. Such weapons were called thrusting swords because of their primary use in battle.

RIGHT:
A two-handed sword,
possibly English, *c* 1450.
Similar weapons have
been excavated near the
site of the battle of
Castillon (1453) in France

TYPES OF NAVAL UNIFORMS.

CHAPTER TWO

SWORDS AT SEA

SWORDS AT SEA

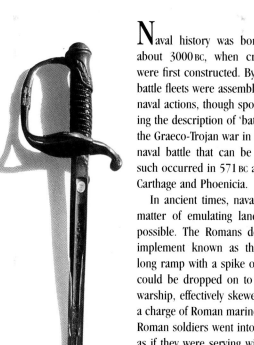

Naval history was born in the Middle East about 3000 BC, when crude river-going crafts were first constructed. By about 1200 BC the first battle fleets were assembled, and the first known naval actions, though sporadic and hardly meriting the description of 'battles', took place during the Graeco-Trojan war in about 1180 BC. The first naval battle that can be positively identified as such occurred in 571 BC and was fought between Carthage and Phoenicia.

In ancient times, naval warfare was largely a matter of emulating land tactics as closely as possible. The Romans depended largely on an implement known as the corvus (grapnel), a long ramp with a spike on the underside, which could be dropped on to the deck of an enemy warship, effectively skewering it and so allowing a charge of Roman marines to capture the vessel. Roman soldiers went into battle aboard ship just as if they were serving with the legions on land. Their equipment differed only a little, although their cloaks were green, while their land-based equivalents wore red.

For centuries naval weapons were similar to those in service on land, and it was not until the middle of the 17th century that distinctive differences in armament appeared and a tradition of naval weaponry began to emerge. The rise of distinctive naval weaponry appears to be contemporaneous with, and may have been a manifestation of, the rise of professionalism in national navies that occurred in the mid-17th century. There is, of course, a well-established brotherhood of the sea, which does not seem to have had its equivalent among land-based forces, and advances and improvements in weaponry were adopted and copied almost as soon as they had occurred. Naval traditions, therefore, tended to overlap and advance simultaneously, even among long-time national foes, and at first, at least, there was little to differentiate the naval weaponry used by different countries. This was especially true of the edged weapons employed by Britain and the US, although after the War of Independence US swords tended to follow French styles more closely. Nevertheless, distinguishing the country of origin of early naval weapons is far from straightforward.

LEFT:
Issued in the 1890s to officers of the Revenue Service, this is often known as the cutter sword. In 1915 this organization merged with the Life Saving Service to form the US Coast Guard.

BELOW:
The standard US Navy cutlass of the Civil War, first adopted in 1860. It was modelled after a French style. It has been reported that some of these weapons were found to be stored on some older American warships as late as the 1930s.

LEFT:
Perhaps the most famous of Elizabeth I's 'sea dogs' was Sir Francis Drake, pictured here by an anonymous artist a few years before the Spanish Armada. Note the incredibly long rapier with the onion-shaped knob and wire-plaited hilt. It is easy to see why the smaller and more manageable smallsword would soon supersede it.

Most national armies achieved uniformity of clothing and armaments before their naval counterparts, but navies soon followed suit. Naval uniforms were adopted in France, later in Spain, some 50 years before they were introduced into the Royal Navy, although a considerable degree of uniformity in dress and equipment had already occurred.

The beginning of the reorganization of the Royal Navy is often credited to Charles II, and many reforms were introduced by his successor and brother, James II. The reorganization was completed by Pitt the younger in time for the French revolutionary wars.

The 18th century dawned with the War of the Spanish Succession (1701–13), Louis XIV's last-ditch gamble to unite the throne of France with that of Spain. This war, which ranged Britain, Austria, the Netherlands, Portugal and Denmark against France, Spain and Bavaria, gave a tremendous impetus to the development of weaponry of all kinds.

Boarding and capturing enemy vessels were the major objectives of navies in the early 18th century. This was partly because cannons were still of dubious value and could not be guaranteed to inflict sufficient damage on an enemy warship to disable it and partly because seizing a prize was an admirable accomplishment in its own right. Even if the captured ship could not be incorporated into the national fleet, which was often the case, the vessel could be dismantled and sold off to help to pay the expenses of the successful navy.

Many European countries adopted the view that the officers' role was to attain a foothold on an enemy vessel and to do what they could to direct their men in the mêlée that ensued. In English-speaking countries the prevailing view seemed to be that officers should lead their men into the thick of a fray and triumph by example. A naval officer, compelled to lead an onslaught across an enemy deck, needed, therefore, a weapon that was both prestigious and functional.

BELOW:
Various dress uniforms of officers in the Royal Navy c 1890. By this time, of course, the sword was strictly a ceremonial object.

TYPES OF NAVAL UNIFORMS.

The John Williamson Company Limited, 42 Gerrard Street, London, W.

Despite what we see in swashbuckling films, however, individual swordfights were virtually unknown. The action was too confused to allow man-to-man confrontations.

As the century progressed, hand-to-hand fighting at sea became more common, and naval officers began to look for serviceable edged weapons, since pistols could still produce only a single shot before being rendered useless. Blades had to be of steel or iron, and, as steel was the more expensive, iron was the more widely used, especially as increasing numbers of edged weapons had to be supplied to enlisted personnel during the wars of the late 18th and early 19th centuries. The handle, known almost universally at sea as the mount, was generally made of brass, although in the interests of economy mounts too were made of iron as more and more swords were needed. Unfortunately, neither metal stood up well to salt air, and mounts and, sometimes, blades, were painted black to protect them.

The first weapon widely adopted by naval officers was a version of the smallsword. It soon proved inadequate, being chiefly effective at thrusting. The blade was too short, and fighting on a pitching, yawing deck required a much longer, more efficient weapon. Smallswords remained regulation wear in the Spanish Navy for several generations, but elsewhere a weapon known as the hanger came into its own and quickly came to be almost universally adopted, especially among naval officers.

At first hangers had comparatively short blades, but they steadily became longer. At the same time, there was a vogue for decorating blades with devices appropriate to the naval service, and it is from these latter weapons, the longer and better engraved hangers, that standardization of naval blades, or fighting swords, as they are more accurately known, may be traced. Hangers were initially more for adornment than anything else. They were frequently known as hunting swords because they were often decorated with scenes depicting fox hunting or the chase. The blade known today as the hunting sword seems to have moved from sea to land during the 17th century. The French developed the sword, turning it into a slightly curved, single-edged blade with a tapering grip. It achieved its greatest popularity in America, and one such weapon that belonged to George Washington may be seen in the Smithsonian Institution in Washington DC.

This version of the hanger remained popular at sea throughout the period of the French Revolution, although the style of decoration changed as more national and naval motifs were adopted. First the mounts and then the blades began to be

SWORD KNOT

Fitting a length of cord to the mount of a sword had become popular at sea by the end of the 17th century. One end of the cord was usually looped over the pommel while the other end was wound around the wrist, so that, if the sword were dropped in the midst of battle, it could quickly be retrieved.

By about 1750 sword knots used in the Royal Navy were blue and gold, and other nations gradually adopted them, selecting colours that were appropriate to the individual service. Eventually, the cord was replaced by gilded wire, which was not only more aesthetically appealing but also stronger.

Although sword knots had been worn by both military personnel and civilians in Britain for many years, there were no regulations pertaining to their style in the Royal Navy for they were considered to be nothing more than ornaments. However, they steadily became more decorative, and by the time of the Napoleonic wars even included tassels. By 1820 the sword knot was an established part of the uniform of the Royal Navy and, by 1827, was enforced by regulation.

The same general trend was followed in America. The blue and gold motif that is still used was quickly adopted, although the use of sword knots was never as widespread as in Britain. In some other European countries, especially Germany, however, they came to be regarded as marks of distinction and were used to indicate not only military achievement but also social status.

ornamented with a range of devices symbolizing the maritime profession. In Britain, for example, the fouled anchor became so widely accepted that it came to be included in dress regulations and was known as the anchor and cable insignia. Other nations followed suit, and soon etchings were engraved on the hilts of naval weapons as a common mark of government ownership.

Throughout Europe and even in America, blades were invariably of German manufacture, for it proved impossible to better the mass-produced and therefore cheap steel blades that were made at places like Solingen. Other accoutrements, such as grips and scabbards, were usually of local domestic make.

In such countries as France, Russia and Spain, army weapons had more influence over naval armaments than in English-speaking countries. Nevertheless, the British Board of Ordnance, which was controlled by the army, held sway over the supply of almost all combat weapons to both services. Thus, it was not until the period of the French revolutionary wars that the blade, which today is identified most closely with naval forces, came into existence.

On both sides of the Atlantic a lightweight sword with a slightly curved blade and large handguard, somewhat resembling a seashell, was soon widely used. The British Army had ordered a new type of lightweight sabre for the cavalry in 1796, and by 1805 it had been copied by British seamen. As early as 1799 American sailors had insisted that this weapon be made available to them, and within a few years this weapon, the cutlass, was accepted as standard in almost every major naval establishment.

Ironically, although the cutlass is indisputably the best known naval edged weapon of all time, it enjoyed a comparatively brief period in favour. Battles by boarding parties were becoming a thing of the past. A few did occur during naval conflicts in the early 1800s, but by the mid-19th century swordfighting was no longer a realistic option. Exploding shells, iron hulls and steam propulsion had made the naval swordfight obsolete. Even so, the short, curved blade of the cutlass remained a common weapon of assassins in the Far East and South America.

As will have become clear, the evolution of naval edged weapons is complex. Each of the major types is discussed briefly below, and the possibility of acquiring each type is assessed.

BELOW:
Marine Corps swords are much scarcer than other types, though they never existed in large quantities. This is of the 1875 pattern. Blade length was usually 68.5–71 cm (27–28 in), with 'USMC' etched on the blade.

RIGHT:
A French sailor of the Napoleonic era, carrying an ornate cutlass. Actually, such weapons were generally only issued as needed for battle, never for dress purposes, so this is obviously a stylized rendering.

CUTLASS

The cutlass still enjoys a certain mystique because of its association with deeds of daring-do, and in literature and the cinema it is traditionally associated with pirates, although, in fact, by the time cutlasses had appeared, the hey-day of pirates was long past.

During the late 18th and early 19th centuries naval fighting swords (see below) had become less and less effective as fighting implements. By 1812 American sailors had begun to use blades with a pronounced curve, especially in the last 30cm (1ft) of their length. This weapon was firmly based on the cavalry sabre, but it was more distinctively designed for use at sea, and it probably reflects the involvement of the US Marine Corps in the wars of the Barbary Coast. The swords were lavishly decorated with heavily embellished hilts; both maritime and patriotic motifs of the day were employed. The size, however, was reduced to a more manageable length, usually no greater than 75cm (30in), and the hilt was shortened in proportion. These swords more closely resembled the Persian scimitar than anything else.

In 1859 the US Marine Corps was ordered to abandon these glamorous weapons and to adopt a pattern of the army regulation sword of 1850. The naval sword was based on a weapon adopted in 1852, and as long as edged weapons were worn as part of the US Navy uniform, it remained virtually unchanged. Officially, the naval weapon had to have a 'cut and thrust' blade approximately 66–74cm (26–29in) long, even though such blades were practically useless at sea. The cutlass was prescribed for enlisted men, and the US Navy's last model of cutlass was adopted in 1860. The enlisted men never wore it unless forced to, however, although it proved popular with officers.

In 1790 a weapon actually designated as a cutlass had been issued in limited numbers in the Royal Navy, although it was not made widely available until 1804. The blade was long and slender but it had a sturdy flat edge, even though the cutting edge was less than ideal. The handguard at the shoulder was wider and stronger than earlier swords, while the knuckleguard almost rolled back on itself from the pommel to the handguard so that it was virtually impossible to lose hold of the weapon through the shock of impact. The hilt was about 11cm (4½in) long,

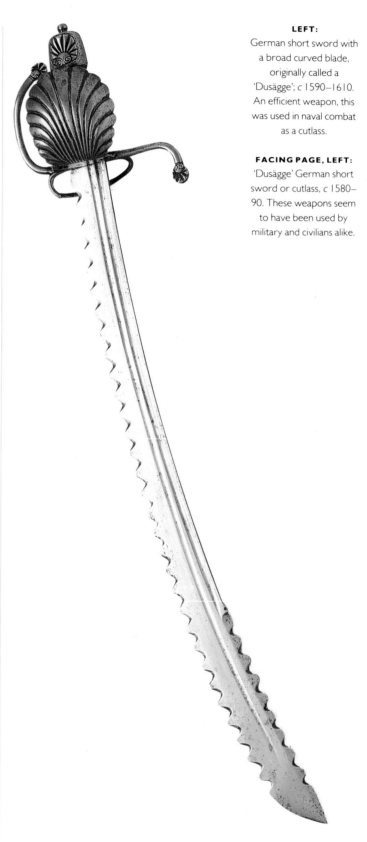

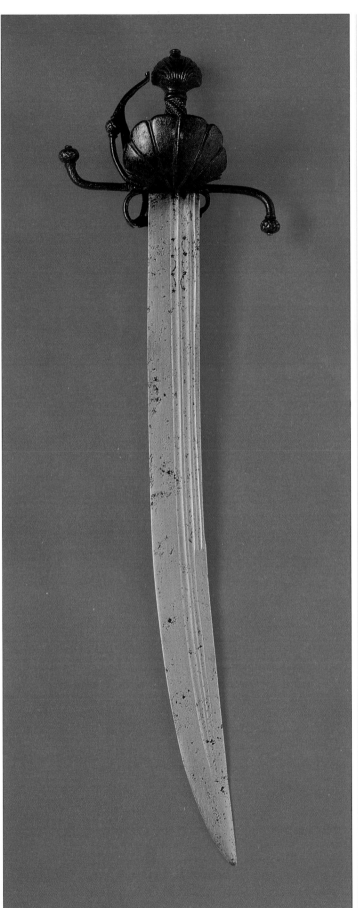

but at 70cm (28in), the blade was still too long for a sword designed for thrusting, and, without some form of curve, it was useless for cutting.

The first regulation 'cutlass' was ordered for the Royal Navy in 1798, but it enjoyed little success, being regarded as nothing more than a poor man's dress sword. Although clearly unsatisfactory in many ways, the Admiralty, among others, encouraged manufacturers to produce it, largely, it seems for reasons of economy. At the time Britain was involved in the Napoleonic wars and needed thousands of weapons. Straight-bladed swords are easier and cheaper to manufacture, and, at a time when mass-production techniques were in their infancy, it is not surprising that the Board of Ordnance did not amend its specifications.

BELOW LEFT:
The last cutlass ever used by the US Navy, which came into service officially in 1917. They were made directly by the US Navy rather than obtained from a contractor, and were, at 60.5–63 cm (24–25 in), shorter than the norm.

BELOW RIGHT:
This German naval cutlass is dated from the middle of the 19th century.

Nevertheless, in 1814 the Board of Ordnance, recognizing that improvements were needed and drawing on the experiences of the Napoleonic wars, issued a new pattern, which was commissioned from Tatham & Egg. Unlike the wicked curve of the American weapon, the blade had a pronounced but smooth curve from the mount to the tip. Length was standardized to a manoeuvrable but dangerous 63–69cm (25–27in), and the first version had a cutting edge of 67cm (26½in). The hilt was also standardized at 13cm (5in), a perfect length. The knuckleguard was no longer oval but began to flare widely in a pear shape to protect as much of the hand as possible. The handguard directly above the shoulder of the blade was expanded for the same reason and became circular.

It is ironic that the ideal weapon for hand-to-hand fighting at sea was developed only at the very end of the time when such combat actually occurred. The cutlass was, in fact, only infrequently used by seamen. The Napoleonic wars were the last conflicts in which laying alongside and boarding enemy ships were a serious element in naval battles.

Acquiring cutlasses does not pose many problems for the collector. British examples are not especially plentiful, largely because they were issued in only limited numbers in the 19th century. US cutlasses are, however, comparatively easy to find. The US Navy was still equipping ships with them as late as 1917, when the US entered World War I, but versions from the Civil War seem to be as easy to find as later ones. Swords that belonged to the US Marine Corps are not easy to find, largely because the Corps was so small at the time of the Civil War; the officers' sword of this period is, in any case, merely a variation of the 1850 US Army pattern. Antiques, dating from the early US campaigns along the Barbary Coast, are, of course, less common and more expensive. Nevertheless, a determined collector will have no trouble in acquiring an interesting and varied selection.

FIGHTING SWORD

By 1770 the naval sword had become transformed into what is known as the fighting sword. The handle was grooved to provide a better grip, and a knuckleguard, usually nothing more than a thin, curved bar attached to a crossguard at the

shoulder of the blade, had been added. The whole weapon was sturdy, and the mount especially was clearly intended as much for combat as for show.

The first weapons were straight and single edged, but by the outbreak of the American War of Independence in 1776 the cutting edge was acquiring a slight curve. Knuckleguards became increasingly elaborate, those of Royal Navy swords often displaying the fouled anchor or lion's head motifs. Blades became shorter: c1750 cutting edges had been as long as 75cm (30in) but by 1770 they were usually no more than 60cm (24in). The reduction in length was purely practical as it was possible to inflict more damage with shorter, more compact blades in the difficult

TOP:
An early US Navy officer's sword, which would usually be made *en suite* with an accompanying dirk. By 1825 it had been supplanted by a much gaudier version, though the carved eagle pommel stayed customary.

CENTRE:
This version of the naval sword was formally adopted in 1852 and, with only minor revisions, remained the standard weapon as long as swords were an official part of the uniform.

conditions prevailing at sea than with longer blades, which were less mobile and more difficult to control. Some people regard this style of fighting sword as the parent of the cutlass, although this view is not widely held.

Straight-bladed weapons did not entirely fall from favour. The officers of most European navies were still carrying such weapons in 1789 at the outbreak of the French Revolution. These blades were long, some more than 75cm (30in) in length, and the grips were equally large at 15–20cm (6–8in). Knuckleguards had become more oval in shape although retaining the 'side ring' appearance. Although they looked impressive, such weapons were already regarded largely

as dress swords and were little used in battle.

By the time the American War of Independence ended in 1783 fighting swords were decorated with gilt and other embellishments. The most popular weapons were those manufactured by James Cullum & Co. of Charing Cross, London, and these swords tended to have shorter blades, less than 75cm (30in) in length, that were slightly thicker and, therefore, stronger in battle.

In 1796 the British Army adopted a standardized sword for its officers. This was based on the Prussian infantry sword that had been carried by the forces of Frederick the Great in the 1740s. The Prussian sword had been similar to the old smallsword (see page 49), but the version

BOTTOM:
A distinctive and quite rare US Marine officer sword, reflecting the influences of the Barbary Coast wars. They were in vogue from about 1825 until the Civil War. The hilt was the pistol-grip design of Arabic weaponry and the blade was usually 76–81 cm (30–32 in).

BELOW:
This weapon dates from *c* 1750, before the American Revolution, as can be seen from the inscribed 'GR' (for George, Rex). It was probably an infantry officer's sword.

BOTTOM:
This weapon is almost exactly a century younger than the one above, though it will be noted that there are few differences. The inscribed 'VR' (or Victoria, Regina) indicates it was 19th century.

adopted by the British Army had a cut and thrust blade that was often as long as 83cm (32½in). The crossguard became heavier and pommels were elaborately decorated. The British Navy followed the Army's lead, and despite its size, this weapon, which was always known as the infantry officer's sword, enjoyed a vogue well into the 19th century. For the first time patriotic inscriptions such as 'for King and Country' were added, mounts were of gilt brass and the hilts were lavishly decorated with maritime motifs. Even among naval officers, however, it was always regarded more as a ceremonial or dress weapon than a fighting implement.

In August 1805 the first recorded regulation pertaining to Royal Naval officers' sword patterns was issued, although it may well have been drawn up earlier. Unfortunately, standardization did not bring an increase in functionalism. The blade was straight edged and slender, which added nothing to its endurance in combat, and the British armed forces seemed unable to free themselves of the belief that longer meant better – blades were 82cm (32in) in length, sometimes longer, and had ponderous mounts and stirrup-style knuckleguards. The hilts became ever more elaborate and frequently bore the lion's head motif. Sword knots became more and more pretentious, and scabbards were splendidly decorated.

In America and in Germany the French version of the fighting sword achieved widespread acceptance. The pattern that was followed *c*1800 had a blade about 75cm (30in) long and a hilt 13–15cm (5–6in) long. It was strikingly different from the British version, although both were based on the light cavalry sabre. The hilts were usually more flamboyant in appearance and tended to slant forwards, which was believed to provide both a better grasp and increase the impact of the blows delivered (there is no evidence that either was, in fact, the case). This style remained popular until the middle of the 19th century.

Fighting swords are not easy to collect. First, comparatively few were made, especially for maritime use. The entire complement of the Royal Navy's officer corps never numbers more than a few thousand men at any time, and, inevitably, many swords were broken or lost at sea over the years. Second, many of these swords were owned by people from families with a naval tradition, and they tended, therefore, to be kept within families as heirlooms. Acquiring such swords is not impossible, however, and dealers and auction houses with contacts in the south of England or on the eastern seaboard of the US are the most likely sources. Prices, however, will reflect this relative scarcity.

FACING PAGE:
Press gangs 'recruited' personnel for both the British Army and Navy. The soldier at right is identified as a regimental sergeant but he seems to be carrying an officer's sword with pronounced pommel, stirrup knuckle-guard and gilt-wire wrapping on the grip.

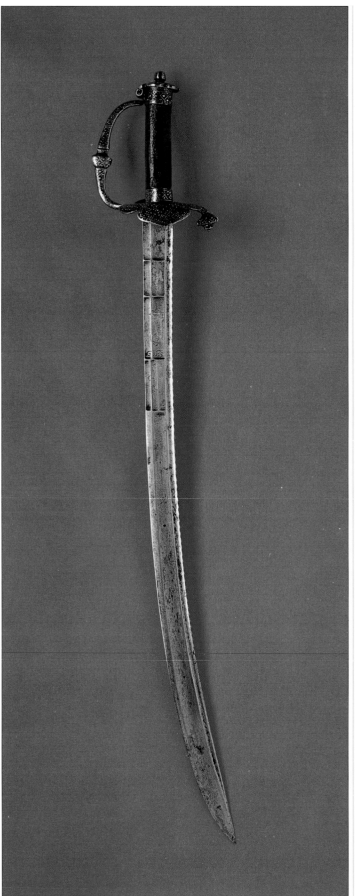

HANGER

The first distinctly recognizable blade was the hanger, so named because it hung from the belt of the wearer. The original hanger was a cheap weapon. It was given little attention in production, and, if scabbards existed, they were roughly crafted leather sheaths. The swords themselves were straightforward, rather flimsy looking. The mounts were usually gilt brass, occasionally even silver, because of the metals' ability to resist corrosion, and they were often decorated with naval motifs; scallop shells were popular, and in some parts of the Caribbean the sword was colloquially called the shell.

The blades were often viewed as something of an afterthought. As with most swords of the period, the blades were usually German in origin, although many were made in Valencia, Spain, which supplied most southern European countries. The blades were slender, often slightly curved and single edged with a straight back away from the cutting edge. Blades were usually 60–69cm (24–27in) long, while hilts were about 15cm (6in) long to allow for maximum grip in action.

LEFT AND BELOW: Single-edged English silver-encrusted hunting hanger (or riding sword) c 1640–50. The fine blade was probably imported from Germany.

ABOVE AND RIGHT:
A hunting sword with etched and gilt single-edged blade by Ambrosius Gemlich of Munich (*c* 1540). The gilt-bronze hilt dates from the 17th century.

As long ago as 1684 Esquemeling, a London writer who specialized in tales of piracy and bloodshed, was illustrating his books with drawings showing hangers used by both pirates and the forces of the law. This is, without doubt, the weapon with which buccaneers were familiar. It is also held to be the first of that series of specialist weapons that 'reached its scientific apotheosis in the cutlass' (*see* P.G.W. Annis, *Naval Swords*).

Collecting hangers can be problematical. They are occasionally found by divers off old pirate strongholds in the Caribbean. In 1986 an old pirate vessel, the *Whyday,* was salvaged off the western coast of Jamaica and several old weapons were recovered and subsequently sold. Auction houses and dealers with contacts in South America or the Caribbean are the most likely sources, although the chances of finding a good quality hanger are not high since the weapons were not particularly sturdy in the first place and tend not to have survived well.

There is the additional problem of actually identifying a hanger as a hanger. The sword was never standardized, and in theory anyone can call an old naval sword an authentic hanger.

HUNTING SWORD

By 1700 the hanger was being transformed into the hunting sword. As we have seen, this had nothing to do with riding to hounds or chasing deer; the sword was named because of the motifs used to decorate it.

The blades of hunting swords were shorter than those of hangers, usually about 50cm (20in) or even less, although the hilts remained a fairly standard 15cm (6in). The curve of the blades became more pronounced.

Hunting swords became popular among British sailors who followed the lead set by Admiral John Benbow. The French version of the sword was widely used on the other side of the Atlantic, where American sailors preferred the more elaborate style, with both longer blades and hilts,

the overall length often being as much as 60cm (2ft). The swords were often embossed with silver, and the scabbards were ornate. The handles tended to be flared, widening towards the pommel. So popular were these swords among American sailors that they were even made in the US by the time of the War of Independence. It is possible to acquire hunting swords today, although they appear on the market only through auction houses or dealers handling the dispersal of private collections. For some reason, few hunting swords are found in the US.

ADMIRAL JOHN BENBOW

The hunting sword was popularized in Britain by John Benbow (1653–1702). He ran away to sea as a boy and joined the Merchant Marine. From 1689 he served in the Royal Navy, seeing action at Beachy Head in 1690 and at Barfleur and La Hogue in 1692, and was Commander in Chief in the West Indies, where, ill-supported by his squadron, he endeavoured to bring the French Admiral to an engagement off Santa Marta. Here, his right leg was shattered by a chain shot, but he returned to the quarterdeck having had his wounds dressed. He died of his wounds at Port Royal. A popular hero in Britain, he was celebrated in Robert Louis Stevenson's *Treasure Island* and honoured by the naming after him of a World War I battleship.

ABOVE AND FACING PAGE: Hunting sword and sheath; the silver hilt is cast and chased with a design showing an American Indian fighting two mountain lions. It was the gift of the Emperor Napoleon III to his friend and fellow collector the 4th Marquess of Hertford (one of the founders of the Wallace Collection in Britain) in about 1860.

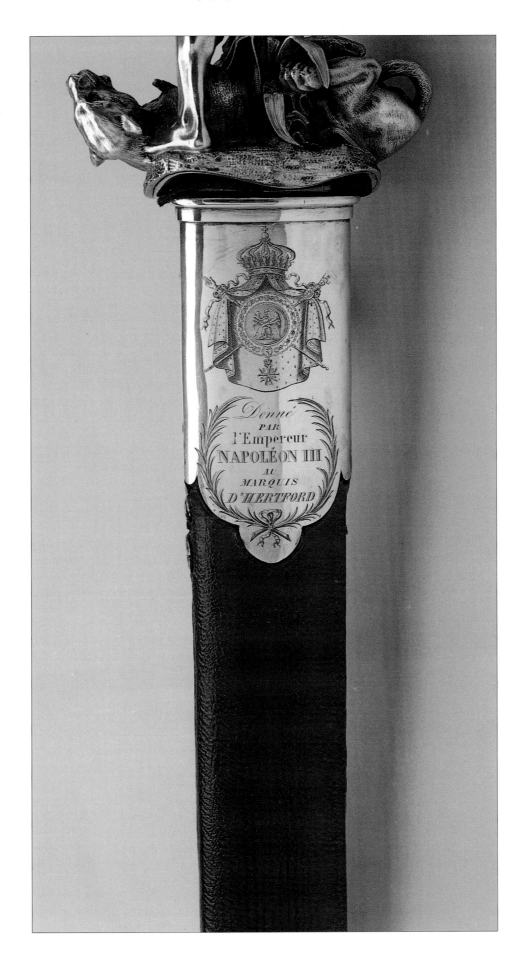

Donné
PAR
l'Empereur
NAPOLÉON III
AU
MARQUIS
D'HERTFORD

NAVAL DIRK

Full-length swords were not the only type of blade found upon the water, but naval dirks are often overlooked in discussions of naval edged weapons. These elongated, elaborate knives first appeared among naval officers at the time of the American War of Independence (1776–83). Originally, many may have been made from broken or no longer useful swords, which could be cut off and new points shaped. The scabbards could be cut down, too, to accommodate the new weapons. They were unofficial and optional, although in the 19th century they were adopted by naval midshipmen on both sides of the Atlantic as something of a regular accoutrement.

Gradually, a tradition developed, especially in the English-speaking navies, of wearing a companion blade to the longer sword. Although this never achieved the status of social custom enjoyed by the Japanese daisho (see page 112), it was a popular trend for many years, and naval dirks began to be manufactured to serve this very purpose. Some US dirks exactly reflect the decorations on the larger companion pieces.

Naval dirks had blades 30–36cm (12–14in) in length and hilts 9–14cm (3½–5½in) in length, although the size of the handle was not as important as the length of the blade. These weapons were never used in anything other than close attack, and there was little need to achieve a fine balance between the mount and blade.

The dirk gained official recognition in the Royal Navy c1800. A blade with a cutting edge some 41cm (16in) in length was produced in very large numbers, probably by Tatham & Egg. This weapon was intended as a symbol of rank, and it was, apparently, regarded as something of a joke by senior commanders. It eventually became standard among midshipmen.

In the US the curved dirk became popular some years before it was accepted in Britain, although it does seem that the Royal Navy long recognized its value as a 'miniature' cutlass. These weapons tended to have longer blades – 38–40cm (15–16in) – but, because of the curve, they were not cumbersome. The hilts gradually became rather over-decorated. In Britain the dirk attained its greatest popularity during the Regency of 1811–20. By c1810 both it and its scabbard were encrusted with gilt and other decorations, including the lion's head motif. US dirks of the same period bore the eagle's head.

A major question that arises in any consideration of the naval dirk is: why were they worn? It would appear that in the Royal Navy, at least, they were actually seen as fighting implements, although they can hardly have been effective when longer and more efficient weapons were used.

LEFT:
This shows a cavalry sabre that has been cut down to a knife, c 1872. Over the eons many swords have been converted in a similar way. It was probably the inspiration for the original naval dirk.

Americans seem to have regarded them as a more convenient way of distinguishing officers while aboard ship than a cumbersome full-length sword. But, in the face of danger, they were abandoned in favour of more powerful blades.

Many otherwise comprehensive collections of edged weapons do not include the naval dirk – perhaps because some collectors feel that they cannot be regarded as serious weapons or because they are put off by the often over-lavish decoration. It is, therefore, possible to find examples comparatively easily.

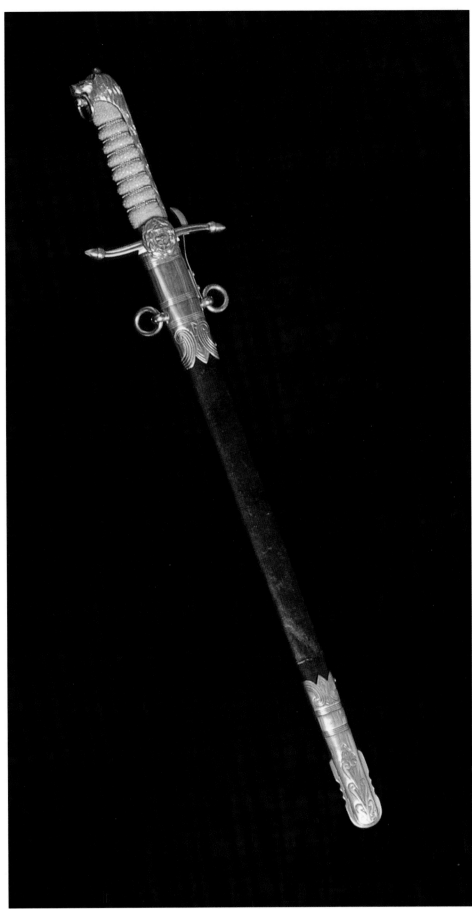

RIGHT:
A Royal Navy midshipman's dirk dating from Victorian times, whose lion's head motif was standard for British objects of the era. The dirk was generally disdained by senior officers and became the symbol of the midshipman.

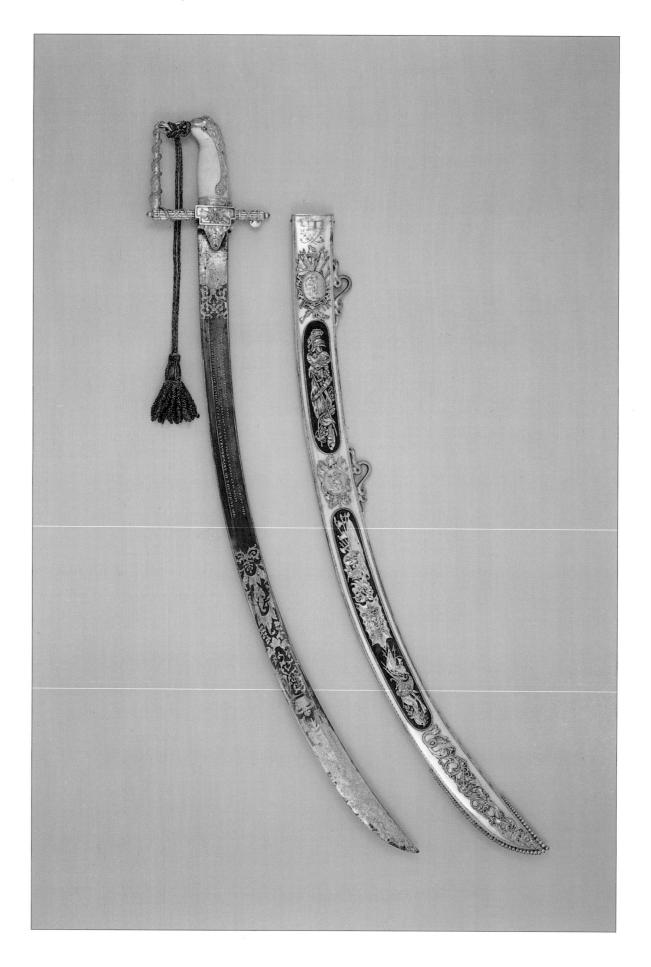

NAVAL SABRE

By 1800 British fighting swords were beginning to acquire curved blades, which seem to have been first made by swordmakers in Birmingham. Hilts were reduced in length to 10–13cm (4–5in), and although knuckleguards were retained and the grips were made of ivory or a similar substance, the swords became less elaborate. Eventually the blades became increasingly curved and shortened to just under 75cm (30in). These swords are known as naval sabres, and they do bear a considerable resemblance to the army equivalent (see page 38), although the naval versions are heavier and somewhat larger.

PRESENTATION SWORD

Although the practice of using naval swords as presentation symbols was much less common than the use of army swords, it was by no means unknown, and was especially popular in Britain and the US, where a substantial number were distributed between c1750 and c1850. These weapons were always a variation of the small-sword (see page 49), which had long fallen from favour as a combat sword.

Many such swords were provided by commercial organizations in the West Indies and India, anxious to demonstrate their approval of, and gratitude to, naval officers who had helped to protect their business interests. The City of London also made several such presentations. Lloyd's of London, the maritime insurance market, itself made 176 such presentations, every

captain of a warship that had fought at the battle of Trafalgar in 1805 being so honoured and receiving the additional and not inconsiderable sum of £100. In 1803 Lloyd's went so far as to establish a Patriotic Fund to 'alleviate the distress' of any dependants of those who would have merited such an award had they survived the event in question.

SPADROON

This curious weapon was first seen in the 1780s. It is sometimes known as the infantry officer's sword of 1786 (see above), but this is, in fact, a misnomer. The weapon was intended to provide both cut and thrust, but it was less than successful. The blades, at 75–82cm (30–32in), were still too long, and, to be effective, thrusting blades must be straight, rigid and relatively compact, like those of the gladii, while cutting blades must be at least partially curved along its major section. The spadroon had a single edge with a straight back, and it was far too long.

Although a British invention, the spadroon was adopted in Scandinavia, Germany and in parts of America. It was never popular in France, where it was known by the derogatory name of the *épée anglais*. The spadroon quickly vanished from naval arsenals. It probably lasted longest in the US Army, where it was still a recommended weapon for infantry officers as late as 1821.

Acquiring a spadroon could be difficult. Most are hard to distinguish from the large fighting swords of the same period – and many are probably sold as such – and, because it was not a successful weapon in itself, few were made.

BELOW AND FACING PAGE:

A good example of the expensive presentation sword distributed by Lloyd's of London in the early 19th century for British military figures who performed exemplary service. The normal cost of such a weapon at the time was not less than 100 pounds sterling. The captain of every ship at Trafalgar received one, but so did many others, and this was awarded to an officer. As it is dated 1811, it was probably for service in Spain against Napoleon. A detail of the inscription is shown below.

OVERLEAF:

A selection of daggers from the 15th and 16th centuries. **CLOCKWISE FROM TOP LEFT:** Venetian ear dagger, c 1500; Landesknecht dagger – German, dating from c 1600 – with steel knife, pricker and sheath; Flemish ballock knife from the mid 15th century accompanied by a sheath, a small knife and a pricker (or steel); German quillon dagger, c 1530; French rondel, c 1440–50.

FROM THE PATRIOTIC FUND AT LLOYDS TO COLONEL CHARLES TURNER OF THE 50TH REGIMENT IN COMMEMORATION OF HIS GALLANT CONDUCT IN SPAIN AS RECORDED IN THE LONDON GAZETTE EXTRAORDINARY OF THE 5TH JUNE 1811

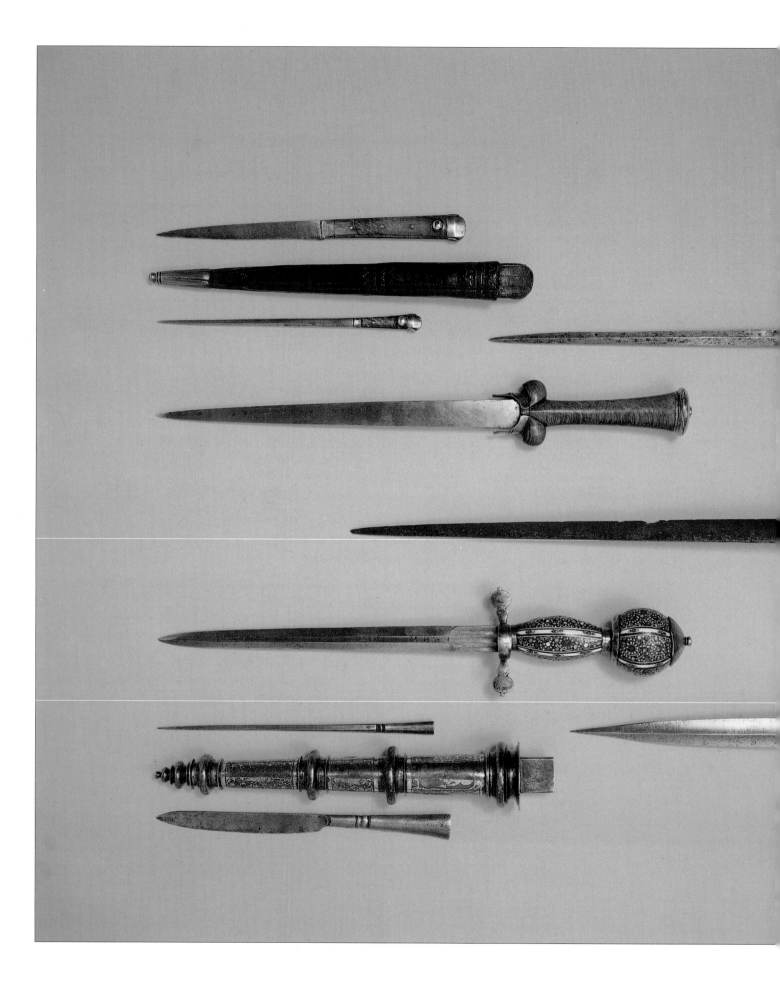

CHAPTER THREE

KNIVES,
DAGGERS AND
DIRKS

KNIVES, DAGGERS AND DIRKS

The small blades of history seem never to have acquired the mystique of larger weapons nor to have attracted the same interest among collectors. Yet, apart from firearms, few weapons have been used to such effect, and even today we see all around us just how dangerous they can be.

The oldest deadly weapon of human history was not, in fact, the sword but the knife, which could be hammered or chiselled or otherwise formed out of almost any substance, although stone was, for obvious reasons, preferred. Even so, the use of the knife in actual fighting is a comparatively recent development. Such implements were used half a million years ago, but primarily for cutting meat, scraping hides or shaping wooden implements, but the Stone Age was almost over before what might be termed a 'fighting knife' appeared.

Ironically, stone knives may have been widely used after metal weapons were developed. In Luristan, an area in northern Mesopotamia along what is today the Iran–Iraq border, excavations have revealed a remarkable culture dating from the 8th and 7th centuries BC. Knives, 56–60cm (22–24in) long, have been found that must have been used for thrusting, although they cannot have been very satisfactory.

Around 1500BC stone knives were widely made and used. Some beautiful knives were made in Ancient Egypt, Africa and Scandinavia,

and Egyptian pieces are among the oldest stone examples still extant. The pale blades, 30–38cm (12–15in) long, had poor tensile strength, and the rear of the blade was usually simply inserted into a handle of wood or, occasionally, ivory, and glued into place. The handle and/or blade was then decorated with scenes depicting the chase. The longer blades must have been purely ceremonial as they were too unwieldy to be used in battle.

In Europe most stone knives were made in Scandinavia. Here, broader and thicker weapons than those made in Egypt were produced, and they continued to be used for longer than elsewhere. In fact, so widespread was the use of stone daggers in Scandinavia, that archaeologists refer to the period 1800–1500BC as the Dolktid (Dagger Period). Blades were made of yellow, amber or brown flint or of black, green, red or white quartzite. The earliest Scandinavian blades seem to have been almost diamond shaped, with one of the long ends somewhat flattened to ensure a better fit with the hilt. Some of the most serviceable Scandinavian stone knives were made between 1600 and 1500BC.

Not all stone knives are ancient however. In the Americas, where the usual stone was obsidian or some similar material, the Aztecs, who first settled in Mexico around 1325, made attractive blades of dark green or black, which was ostentatiously decorated. As recently as a century ago, moreover, Indian peasants could make dozens of obsidian blades a day by holding the stone in the feet and flaking away the material. No tool was needed: a skilled artisan could create blades by peeling off chunks using his body weight against the obsidian.

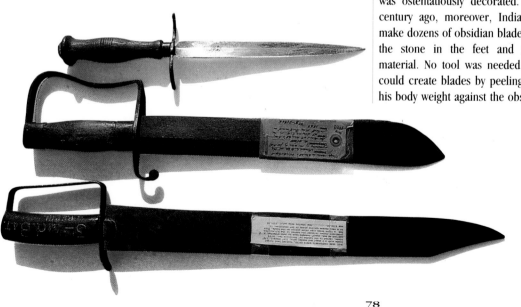

However, stone implements have always suffered from one major problem: although relatively sharp edges could be achieved, once chipped and broken they could not be repaired or resharpened. As we have already seen, copper was among the first metals to be used in the making of weapons. However, copper is malleable, and blades had to be thick or wide or both to withstand any kind of impact, and it was almost impossible to produce a serviceable blade longer than about 15cm (6in).

To overcome this problem, blades were initially made parallel for most of their length from the handle, tapering to a point. This ogival shape was an improvement but not sufficient to provide long-lasting weapons. Attempts to make copper weapons larger with the tang as a single piece made them more prone to snap on impact. Adding a central rib made the blade stronger, producing a stiffer, thicker weapon, and these were made in two-piece moulds.

The discovery of bronze allowed more durable blades to be made, although the smelting process was rather haphazard and produced bronzes with anything from 2 to 20 per cent tin, the greater the proportion of tin, the stronger the blade. Metal hilts were also made, which overcame the problem of the weak point where the handle was attached to the blade. Grips were made of ivory or bone – some pearl grips have

been discovered – pommels grew more complex in terms of design.

The Bronze Age reached Europe along the trade routes of the rivers Danube and Elbe, and bronze daggers from the Dolktid Period have been found in Scandinavia. Weapons dating from this period were not intended to be works of art. Grips were cylindrical, and pommels were flat and plain. by 1400BC they were being cast as a single unit in places as diverse as northern Italy, the Rhone valley in France and central Germany. When not cast as a solid piece with the blade, the handle was usually riveted. Half a dozen small rivets were usually sufficient, although some Bronze Age pieces from Wiltshire in southern England have as many as 32 rivets.

Among the finds at Hallstatt in upper Austria, which are thought to represent a transitional period between the Bronze and Iron Ages, were found knives of bronze, frequently overlaid with gold; both the blade and scabbard of one of the daggers were even overlaid with gold leaf. The best know example has been called the 'key grip' because it resembles a house key. Pommels were fashioned into stylized human faces. The finds at La Tene in France, which date from c500BC, reveal that knives had fallen from favour, for they are mostly single-edged blades. The daggers had come to resemble butcher's knives with a straight back and a blade that curved slightly to the tip.

From this period, for almost a thousand years, the dagger was more or less consigned to oblivion. The Roman war machine was based on the gladius, and even senior commanders spurned the dagger for ceremonial purposes.

It was not until Charlemagne instituted the *hari bannus* (the hereban) that daggers returned to favour. In time of war, the king had the right to levy and lead the host, but the Frankish kingdoms over which Charlemagne ruled were so extensive that the king could not carry out his military duties without delegating them to men trained in the use of arms. The counts' powers of *bannus* were derived from the king's, and the counts were the king's lieutenants in administrative districts small enough to be supervised by one man. Within each district, groups of men were made responsible for providing individual soldiers with equipment for war, and among the implements each soldier was expected to carry was a sword, shield, spear and dagger.

This group of edged weapons – whether used for fighting, self-defence or outright assassination – is one of the largest, and limitations of space mean that only some of the most distinctive or important may be considered here.

BASELARD

One of the most popular and widespread daggers was the baselard, which is, it is thought, so named because it was invented in Basle, Switzerland; it is the forerunner of the Swiss dagger (see below). The baselard first appeared at the end of the 13th century. It was longer than most daggers – sometimes almost as long as a short sword – and a simple but sturdy crosspiece and pommel give it a distinctive appearance, the entire handle resembling a capital I. The blades tapered evenly to a point, and the grips were made of two pieces of, usually, horn, wood or ivory, riveted together. The baselard was used by people in all walks of life, including knights.

These daggers can be collected today, and, naturally, are most likely to be found through European auction houses and dealers.

BOWIE KNIFE

Tradition has it that in 1830 Colonel Jim Bowie of Logan County, Kentucky, visited a knifemaker named James Black in Arkansas. He wanted a special blade made with which he could skin animals, although whether it was designed by Bowie himself or by his brother Rezin is still open to debate. Black studied Bowie's prototype, made some adjustments and then allowed that he could make something worthwhile. What transpired was the most famous blade in US history, the Bowie knife or Arkansas toothpick.

Bowie did not intend the knife to be used for fighting, although it was, in fact, used in more murders and duels in American history than any weapon apart from the pistol. Bowie himself probably used his knife to kill a few men, including a number of Mexicans at the Alamo, but the number is probably exaggerated.

The Bowie knife is single edged, with a straight, powerful back, a sharp point and a blade curving gently to meet it. Bowie had wanted the blade to be 30–33cm (12–13in) long, but Black shortened it to 25cm (10in); later, the blade was even shorter than that.

By the middle of the 19th century the Bowie knife's fame had spread, and a number of companies as far afield as Sheffield in northern England were manufacturing them. Ultimately, more Bowie knives were manufactured in Britain than in the US.

Today the Bowie knife is regarded as the quintessential American weapon. However, many fakes have been made over the years, and collectors should make sure that they purchase only examples with the name of the original owner engraved on the handle or on the shoulder of the blade, which was commonly done in the 19th century. It is, moreover, possible to trace, through records in public libraries and local genealogical groups, whether the individual supposed to have owned the knife actually existed. Historic examples with established provenances are rarely offered for sale, and when they are, they are expensive.

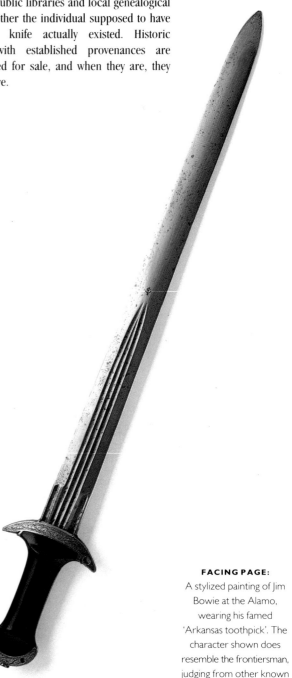

BELOW:
The baselard is traditionally Swiss in origin. This example dates from c 1530.

FACING PAGE:
A stylized painting of Jim Bowie at the Alamo, wearing his famed 'Arkansas toothpick'. The character shown does resemble the frontiersman, judging from other known portraits of Bowie.

CINQUEDEA

In northern Italy in the late 15th century smiths at Villa Basilica first made a weapon that more closely resembled a small sword than a dagger. This was the cinquedea, whose name stems from the fact that its savage blade, somewhat like an oversized garden trowel, was five fingers wide at the shoulder. The wide and sweeping quillons were decorated with mythological motifs.

Original cinquedeas are extremely rare, most now being in museums, and many fakes were produced, especially in Milan in the 1840s. Acquiring a cinquedea should be done only through a reputable dealer. Equally rare are examples of the original scabbards, which were elaborately decorated, leading one London museum to describe them as 'the finest pieces of art in leather known'.

BELOW AND FACING PAGE:
Italian 'Cinquedea', a dagger or short sword for civilian wear (c 1500), with its original *cuir bouilli* (hardened leather) sheath. There is a pocket at the back for a by-knife.

LEFT:
The 'Cinquedea' – whose name comes from the 'five-fingers' breadth of the blade – was carried across the buttocks. This example, dating from c 1480, probably comes from Ferrara, Italy.

COMMANDO KNIFE

The modern commando or combat knife is not normally included in discussions of edged weapons, more attention being lavished on more expensive and exotic knives. A combat knife is, strictly, a weapon designed to be used as a sidearm; it is not an all-purpose tool. Cutting implements such as pangas, bolos and machetes are not fighting knives. The true fighting knife is designed to be carried in the belt and is, therefore, rarely longer than 15–20cm (6–8in) or wider than 3cm (1¼in).

The best known examples are currently out of favour. In World War I the trench knife was most widely used; it was double edged and had a set of brass knuckles as a handguard. It is too bulky and awkward to gain general acceptance today. In World War II, the best known weapon was the British-made Fairbairn-Sykes commando knife, a variant of which was popular with US Marines in the Pacific. Unfortunately, this weapon proved to be too brittle to survive being used to open letters or take the tops off bottles of beer – the kind of things US soldiers used their knives for – and an American named Walter Doane Randall invented what many regard as possibly the best fighting knife yet. The blade, which was made of high-carbon steel, was 17–20cm (7–8in) long and 6mm (¼in) thick, and it had a modest sweep to the tip of the single edge. For strength and manoeuvrability it has not been bettered.

Today there are two main types of commando knife. One is broad, flat and double edged; the other resembles a stiletto. Many have a hole in the pommel or handle through which a leather thong can be passed and slipped over the wrist to prevent the knife being inadvertently dropped.

Building up a collection of combat knives might prove to be one of the easiest types of collection to amass. Almost any military surplus store should have examples, and some stores specialize in them. However, having begun with recent knives, many collectors will then wish to widen their scope and extend into antique and historical versions; these can prove expensive and more difficult to acquire.

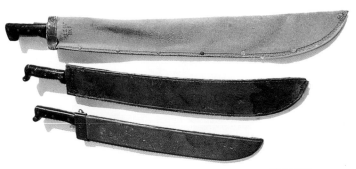

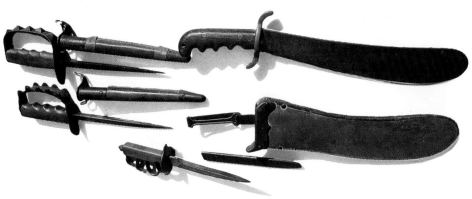

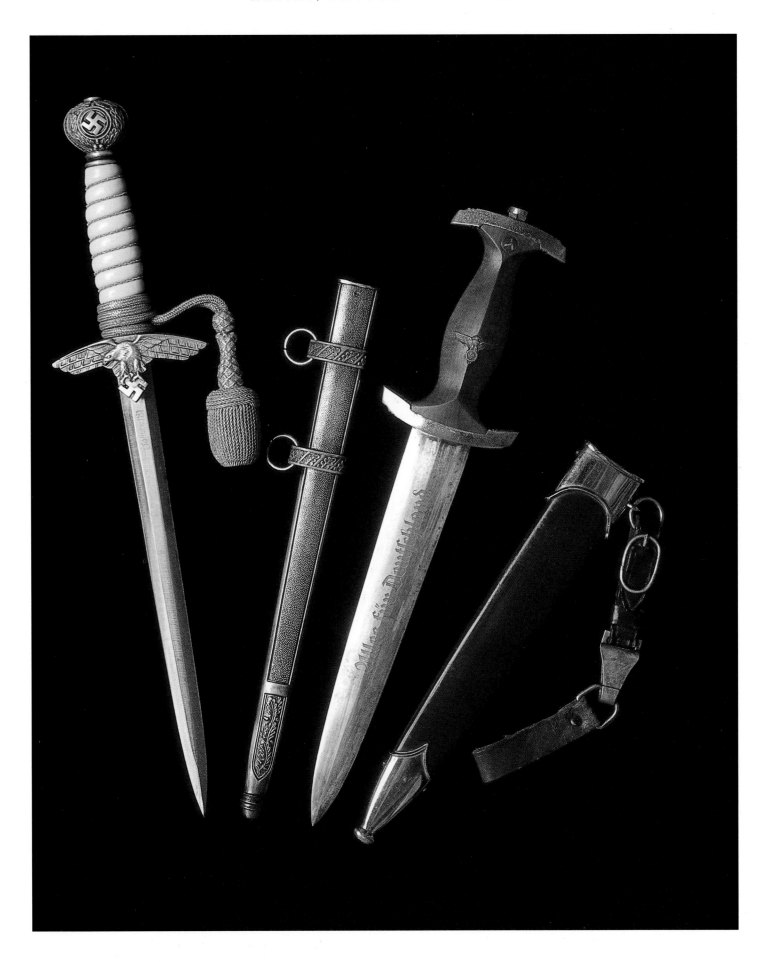

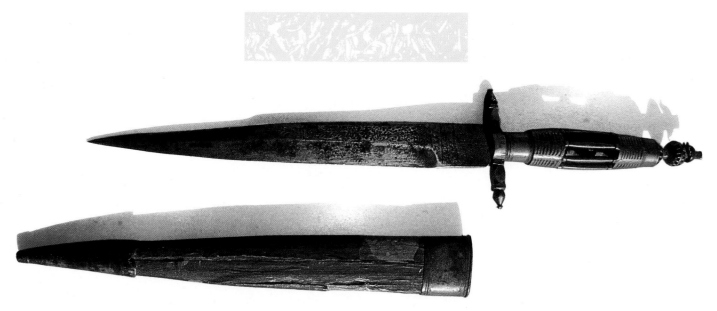

DIRK

One of the most misunderstood of fighting knives is the dirk. Its immediate forerunner was the Scottish ballock knife, which was known by that name and widely used by the 14th century although it had been developed earlier, its antecedents going back to 1050AD, if not before. The short-bladed ballock knife was kept in a low-slung sheath, hung from a belt, and carried between the thighs – which appears to have been the origin of its name. The prudish Victorians called it the kidney knife, but by this time the original ballock knife had been transformed into an implement known as a dudgeon dagger.

In the 17th century a longer bladed knife appeared, and by 1650 this was universally known as a 'durk'. The knife's origins are obscure, but the spelling now current appears to be the result of an error by Dr Johnson when he included the word in his dictionary in 1755. By c1700 blades were about 38cm (15in) long – almost as long as a small sword – while the single cutting edge tapered to the tip and the hilts were usually made of pewter or brass. By the middle of the century the dirk had become more elaborate. The grips were wrapped in silver wire, and the pommels were dome shaped. The blades had broadened shoulders, known as haunches,

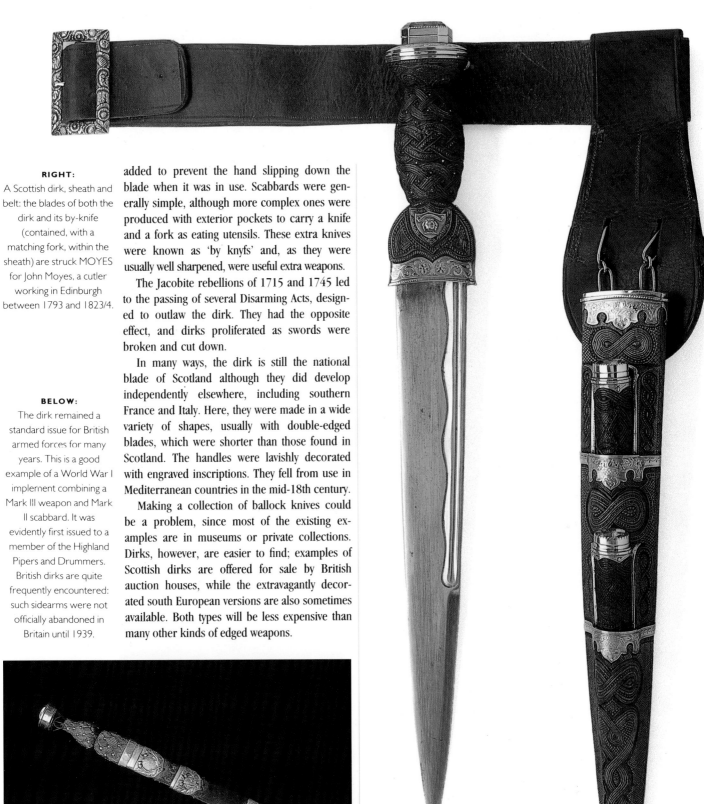

added to prevent the hand slipping down the blade when it was in use. Scabbards were generally simple, although more complex ones were produced with exterior pockets to carry a knife and a fork as eating utensils. These extra knives were known as 'by knyfs' and, as they were usually well sharpened, were useful extra weapons.

The Jacobite rebellions of 1715 and 1745 led to the passing of several Disarming Acts, designed to outlaw the dirk. They had the opposite effect, and dirks proliferated as swords were broken and cut down.

In many ways, the dirk is still the national blade of Scotland although they did develop independently elsewhere, including southern France and Italy. Here, they were made in a wide variety of shapes, usually with double-edged blades, which were shorter than those found in Scotland. The handles were lavishly decorated with engraved inscriptions. They fell from use in Mediterranean countries in the mid-18th century.

Making a collection of ballock knives could be a problem, since most of the existing examples are in museums or private collections. Dirks, however, are easier to find; examples of Scottish dirks are offered for sale by British auction houses, while the extravagantly decorated south European versions are also sometimes available. Both types will be less expensive than many other kinds of edged weapons.

LEFT:
A left-hand dagger, made
of steel, with a silver wire-
bound grip. It is possibly
German, c 1610–20.

HAUSWEHREN

Many edged weapons are associated with members of the knightly class or nobility, but peasants were also armed. In almost every country in Europe there was a type of blade known today by the German name hauswehren, which is appropriate, for the weapons were indeed intended for the defence of the home. Although they were simple, hauswehren should not be thought of as ordinary pocket knives – they more closely resembled butcher's knives, and although they were officially regarded as working knives, they could also be used as effective weapons.

Some writers have suggested that hauswehren are derived from the Viking scramasax (see below), while others have propounded the less likely theory that they are the forerunner of the Bowie knife (see above).

The knives were popular from the 7th to the 17th century, and it should, therefore, be possible to obtain several examples, since it seems likely that there are many in junk shops and second-hand shops throughout Europe. Acquiring a large collection might, however, be a question less of cost than of personal taste.

LEFT-HAND DAGGER

Despite its name, the left-hand dagger was not a weapon specifically made for left-handed people. It was a companion piece for the rapier, and for many years it was held to be correct to defend with the rapier and to strike with the left-hand dagger. The dagger was usually made as a pair with the sword, and the two have been widely described as 'the only right and true gentlemanly weapons'. The dagger had a stiff, straight blade and was usually as gaudily decorated as the rapier, especially around the knuckleguard. The two weapons were popular from the early 16th until the late 17th century, and in Spain they continued to be used until the 18th century.

Examples of left-hand daggers are rarely seen outside museums; rapiers are far easier to acquire. Nevertheless, it is still possible to find left-hand daggers through dealers based in southern Europe and, if you are prepared to travel, in the major cities of South America.

NAVAJA

This, the Spanish clasp knife, dates from at least the 15th century and was made by cutlers in a dozen cities in Spain. It was the forerunner of the switchblade knife (flick-knife), its slightly oval blade folding into the handle.

The first manual to discuss fighting with knives concerns the navaja. It was written in 1849 by someone known only as M. d. R., who was probably a disinherited Italian or Spanish aristocrat. The manual was aimed at the working classes, and the author made frequent derogatory comments about the 'so-called decent class' and named knifefighters *barateros*. The navaja was usually used to slash at an opponent, but M. d. R. wrote that any tactic that gained the advantage was acceptable. If all else failed, he wrote, throw the knife at your opponent to give yourself time to escape through the window.

Versions of the navaja are still used throughout the Spanish-speaking world, and a persistent collector could acquire a considerable number. Although it would not be possible to establish an historic provenance for each weapon, they would form a fascinating group.

QUILLON

The quillon, which is simply a small version of a sword, can be traced back to the Hallstatt culture, the Celtic civilization representing the transition between the Bronze and Iron Ages. The blades taper evenly, the pommels are round or crescent shaped, and the crossguards are solid.

The dagger appeared in its present form in the 13th century. It was primarily a knightly weapon, and was worn suspended from the belt by a ring through the pommel; this gave rise to its alternative name, the ring dagger. Like the knightly class, the quillon had fallen from favour by 1500.

Many quillons undoubtedly exist in private collections throughout central Europe, and it is possible that a specialist dealer might be able to acquire one. However, because of their association with knights, they are expensive.

RONDEL DAGGER

The rondel dagger originated at the same period in history as the ballock knife (see above), but it was used in southern Europe. The pommel was formed of two solid discs of wood, and a long tang ran through the blocks and was riveted to form the grip.

In the 14th century an interesting version of the rondel appeared. This was the eared dagger, which shares its heritage with the blade known to the Turks as the yataghan and to the Cossacks as the shashqa. The pommel of eared daggers was split in two (with the result that many resemble badly formed images of Mickey Mouse) to allow the thumb to be hooked over the pommel to impart greater force to the stabbing blow. Curiously, despite its appearance, the eared dagger became widely associated with royalty and it was also a favourite weapon with assassins in Italy in the 15th and 16th centuries.

SCRAMASAX

The all-purpose knife used by the Vikings who raided and settled the coasts of Britain and western Europe in the 8th and 10th centuries was the scramasax. In fact, this knife did not originate in Scandinavia but had been used by the ancient Franks and by the Germanic hordes which had harried and eventually replaced the Roman Empire, France and Britain respectively in the 4th and 5th centuries. Nevertheless, it was the Vikings who made this knife their own. Scholars are of the opinion that the word *sax* refers to sword and that *scrama* means 'a wound-making implement'; the word may, therefore, be translated rather tautologically as 'wound-making sword'.

The scramasax has, in a masterpiece of understatement, been described as a 'sturdy knife'. The blades were anything from 10 to 50cm (4–20in) long, but all were single edged and triangular in cross-section. The back of the blade ran parallel to the edge, usually tapering only at the end to meet the tip. The handles were broad and riveted just below the pommel, which was round or onion shaped, while the grips were made of leather or wood.

It remained in favour in Europe for several centuries, being used in Scandinavia until the 12th century, while a variant was carried in England as late as the 15th century. The scramasax, therefore, represents something of a transition between Iron Age daggers and the more sophisticated fighting knives with which we are familiar today.

RIGHT:
A rondel dagger, possibly French, from c 1450. Similar brass studs have been found on a rondel dagger recovered from the Thames.

LEFT:
Rondel or 'ear' dagger, Venetian or Spanish, dating from c 1500. It would have been held point downwards, with the thumb lying over the top of the grip, between the 'ears'.

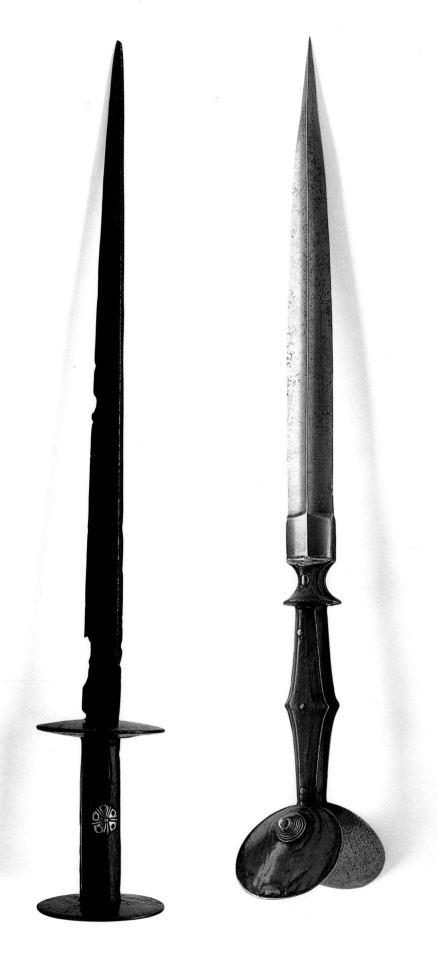

STILETTO

The weapon known as the stiletto first gained favour in the 16th century and remained popular for about 150 years. It was a smaller version of the stilo (Italian dagger), and the stiletto's stiff blade, somewhat triangular in cross-section, made it really useful only when used with a stabbing motion. The hilt was usually steel with a simple crossguard.

Stilettos became popular in southern Europe when edicts forbidding weapons to be carried were passed; the slim daggers could be easily hidden in clothing. They could also be hidden inside hollow staffs, known as brandestocs, a practice that was widespread in Europe. Stilettos were also often carried by artillery troops because the scales for measuring powder charges were engraved on the scabbards.

Although it was not an especially effective weapon, the stiletto has acquired a reputation for being used to commit murders and assassinations. They were made in all shapes and sizes, and it is not too difficult to find examples, although they will be expensive.

RIGHT:
Stiletto, made entirely of chiselled steel; Italian (Brescian), dating from c 1650.

BELOW:
Stiletto, probably West European, dating from the early 17th century.

SWISS DAGGER

The Swiss dagger is sometimes confused with the schweizerdegen (the Swiss short sword), and it is a truly large and brutal-looking weapon. It is also known as the holbein, after the painter Hans Holbein the younger, who produced a series of wood engravings entitled *The Dance of Death*, motifs from which were frequently engraved on Swiss daggers. The daggers were usually flamboyantly decorated, and the scabbards were festooned with designs depicting scenes from folklore. The Swiss dagger is the prototype of the German SS dagger, which was first issued in 1936 (see below). Many of these were highly decorated, and scabbards were often inscribed with the SS motto *Meine Ehre Heisst Treue* (My Honour is Loyalty).

In their original form, Swiss daggers are extremely difficult to acquire. Similar weapons are obtainable, however, as are the SS daggers.

BELOW:
Swiss dagger or holbein *c* 1560; the gilt-copper sheath depicts the Legend of Virginia, with Appius Claudius III on the Judgement Seat. The dagger itself, though stylistically correct, is a 19th-century replacement.

FAR LEFT:
Swiss dagger (possibly German) dating from *c* 1600, with encrusted silver decoration.

ABOVE LEFT:
The German army's all-purpose knife was also a dagger – and a fine weapon. However, they were never regarded as very useful in blitzkrieg warfare, and were most often employed for an assortment of non-combat functions.

ABOVE RIGHT:
The Nazi Luftwaffe dagger was issued in large numbers to German paratroopers in World War II.

THIRD REICH DAGGERS

No discussion of daggers and knives would be complete without reference to the edged weapons produced during the Third Reich. Most of these weapons were purely ceremonial and were produced as a sop to Hitler's passion for the trappings of the Reich and Naziism. Swords, for example, were commonly borne on dress occasions, although they were never seriously considered to have any military value.

Daggers, however, were another matter. They played a prominent part in the riots that brought Hitler to power in 1933, and the SS (Schutzstaffel) knives, first issued in 1936, were efficient weapons, even though they were often intricately decorated, with silver handles and ivory or burnished horn inlays. The German paratroopers and commandos under Skorzeny used knives to great effect.

Despite the popularity of Nazi weapons, it is still not difficult to acquire blades from that era, especially some of the smaller types. However, there is a view that these weapons are overpriced, and even though building a modest collection would not be impossible, there is always the possibility that the allure of the Third Reich will, in time, pass from fashion.

RIGHT:

A German sentry guarding the fortifications along the coast of France sometime during World War II. Note the bevy of dress daggers with which he is kitted out. This is almost certainly a staged shot. The average German infantryman would have had no particular need for one such weapon, much less several.

BELOW:

A detail showing the handle of the Third Reich Luftwaffe dagger, seen in full on page 85.

RIGHT:
A German propaganda/recruiting poster for the U-boat service. A submarine officer obviously had no need for a dagger except on rare ceremonial occasions. However, it was in keeping with the stealthy, silent strike that symbolized the 'sea wolves'.

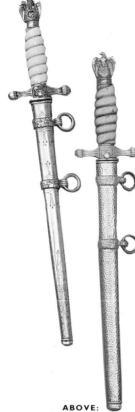

ABOVE:
Two variants of the naval dress dagger. German forces commanders were well aware of the important morale-boosting qualities of such uniform 'extras'.

FAR RIGHT:
German World War II daggers were allotted on the basis of service and rank. Here we see a 1937 pattern Luftwaffe dagger in the context of an Oberleutnant's uniform and other memorabilia. Note (below), by way of contrast, the uniform of a 2nd Panzer Regiment officer.

Freiwillig zur
KRIEGSMARINE

CHAPTER FOUR

EDGED
WEAPONS
FROM THE EAST

EDGED WEAPONS FROM THE EAST

Distance lends enchantment, of course, but the military customs and weapons of the Orient and subcontinent of India have long fascinated the Western world. Recently that fascination has been fed by various broadcasting media, but there are still enormous gaps in our knowledge of the history and customs of the area, and this ignorance seems to have added to, rather than diminished, the interest shown by collectors of militaria in the artefacts produced in Asia and India.

The military tradition in Japan is probably the best known, and some Japanese edged weapons are discussed later in this chapter. Other nations too, however, had complex and remarkable military histories.

ABOVE:
Early 19th-century Chinese sword with a carved jade hilt and scabbard of *cloisonné* enamel.

China produced one of the great military philosophers in Sun Tzu, and the art of warfare was well advanced there by the 6th century BC. However, weaponry seems to have been of only moderate quality, the military strength depending more on the number of chariots available. Chinese soldiers appear to have been valued more for their numbers than for their individual skills, and this *ad hoc* approach produced few edged weapons of interest, the arms varying widely from region to region.

The current regime's attitude to the West makes it unlikely that we will have an opportunity at least in the foreseeable future, to study the nation's ancient military structure and weaponry. Among the weapons that would be of interest are the Chinese execution swords, especially those used by the Manchu dynasty (1644–1912) at the beginning of this century. Also of interest would be the smaller blades used by Chinese soldiers, both from the mainland and from Taiwan, and it is just possible that a specialist dealer might be able to acquire examples.

FACING PAGE:
An engraving by Zafar-Nama dated 1548, entitled *Shiraz Tumur's Invasion of India.*

LEFT:
Late 18th-century (Ch'ing dynasty) Chinese sword. The mounts are of gilt copper and the scabbard is covered with green ray skin.

A word that has become synonymous with military might is Mongol. The name first appeared in Chinese records of the 6th century, and the power of the tribe from east-central Asia reached its zenith under Genghis Khan, who became emperor in 1206, and his grandson, Kublai Khan (1216-94), the first Mongol emperor of China. The basic fighting unit of the Mongols was the touman, a 10,000–strong group, and, despite the Mongol 'hordes' of legend, it seems that only rarely did more than a dozen toumans ride out together. Their success was due to the use of signal flags, careful strategy, fanatical courage and the fact that the Mongols as a race were inured to hardship.

Although they were horsemen, the preferred arms were the bow, javelin and lasso, although they did carry a weapon, poorly depicted in ancient illustrations, that resembled a small scimitar or large sabre. This weapon may, in fact, be the forerunner of the Indian talwar (see below), but few edged weapons have ever been attributed to the Mongols and those are all in museums.

INDIA

The military heritage of the subcontinent of India can be traced back to the original Aryan invasions that occurred between c2000 and 1000BC. These settlers from central Asia moved into the Punjab and the upper valley of the Ganges, bringing with them the rudiments of Hindusim. The subcontinent, apart from the far south, was united under the Mauryan emperors (321–184BC), but the area was not unified again until the era of the Gupta dynasty (AD300–500), whose rule was ended by the raids of the White Huns, which plunged India into anarchy. During the 11th and 12th centuries India suffered invasions from Moslems, Turks, Arabs and Afghans, and in 1206 the first Moslem dynasty was established, and was followed by three centuries during which Moslem rule was confirmed throughout the north and the Deccan. In the 14th–16th centuries the south remained independent under the Hindu Vijayanagar dynasty. In 1527 began the greatest period of Moslem India with the founding of the Mogul empire by Babur, but after 1707 the empire, although officially lasting until 1858, fell into decline and a further period of anarchy ensued. It was at this time that traders from Portugal, Holland, France and Britain had begun to establish outposts in India, and the Seven Years War (1756–63) gave the East India Company the opportunity to oust the French and install itself as a master of Bengal and the Carnatic. Within a century, British rule, direct or indirect, was established throughout the entire subcontinent.

Although India has, therefore, seen more than its fair share of warfare, technologically the subcontinent appears to have lagged behind other areas. Iron weapons did not appear until c500BC, and chariots, augmented with, but never supplanted by, elephants, were the basis of military strength. The infantry was largely composed of bowmen, and India's greatest military treatise, *Siva-Dhanur-Veda*, which appeared around AD500, concentrated on archers. Hand-to-hand

ABOVE:
A set of fakir's horns, clearly showing the metal tips projecting from the horns of bone.

conflict was on the whole avoided, and by AD200 Hindu conflict was conducted along essentially ritual lines, with limited objectives sought and mass-slaughter avoided.

Nevertheless, despite the constraints imposed by Hindu attitudes to warfare, an astonishing number of interesting edged weapons was produced in the subcontinent, and several of these are discussed below. There were also some oddities. One of the most curious was the bagh nakh,

meaning tiger's claw, a five-pronged weapon that slipped over the hand like brass knuckles but that was made deadly by the spikes. Another unusual implement was the fakir's horns, a type of weapon seen only in India. Holy men were prevented by law from carrying real weapons but found it necessary to protect themselves. A pair of animal horn blades would be fastened together so that they pointed in opposite directions, and metal tips were added, making a useful, if non-lethal, weapon for close-quarters or darkness.

Collecting weapons from the Indian sub-continent used not to be difficult. Most of the maharajahs had built up extensive collections, and dealers and even tourists could acquire examples almost at will. This is still possible as some of the weapons are still being made. Prices, however, have increased steeply, and it is probably essential to use the services of a dealer with contacts in the area. Among the most desirable of Indian weapons are the bichwa, the khanjarli and the pata.

BHUJ

The characteristic Hindu dagger of northern India is known as the bhuj or kutti, and it is also called the elephant knife, as that motif was used as decoration. The single-edged blade was comparatively heavy although only 17–25cm (7–10in) long. A decorative knob served as a pommel. The bhuj was unusual in so far as its long tang could be screwed into a hollow hilt, thereby transforming the blade into a sword up to 60cm (2ft) long.

BICHWA

The word bichwa means 'sting of the scorpion', and this dagger has attracted a certain amount of legend as it was the preferred weapon of assassins. The blade was formed in the configuration of a buffalo horn, and a steel hilt was usually looped around to make a knuckleguard and to afford greater strength and security. The blade length was 25cm (10in). Bichwa came into popular use in the 17th century, though it was used earlier. They are still in use today.

JAMBIYA

This single-edged knife is one of the more attractive weapons. The blade was often inlaid with gold, jade or ivory, and the wooden sheaths, which tended to be much longer than the blades, were embossed with leather or silk. The knife was the symbol of a free man, and to have it taken away meant irredeemable degradation. The Jambiya blade could be anything from 12cm (5in) to 25cm (10in) in length. Shorter models were preferred in India; the longest found were used by the Berbers in Morocco. These weapons are still manufactured, though are now for ornamental purposes only.

KARD

This single-edged, rather unpretentious weapon could be anything from 20 to 40cm (8–16in) long. The tip was thickened to increase the effectiveness of the blow. The grip was of bone or horn, and the straight hilt had no handguard.

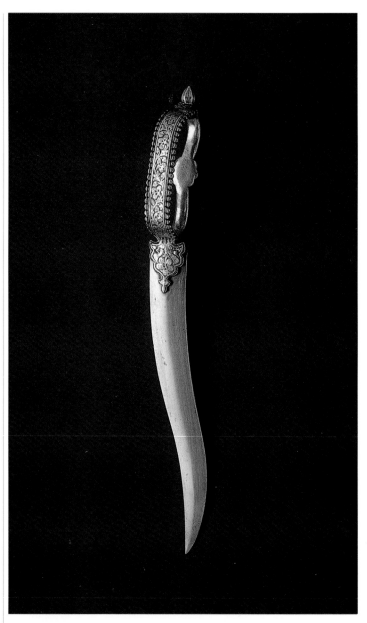

KHANDA

If India can be said to have a national sword it is the khanda. It has a long, straight blade with a blunt point. The blade was generally single-edged and was wider at the tip. The padded grip inclined forwards slightly, and a curved spike formed a pommel, allowing the khanda to be used in much the same way as the European bastard sword (see page 30). The sword could be up to 75cm (30in) long.

KHANJAR

The khanjar is, like the talwar (see below), of Moslem origin, and some variant of the word means knife in several languages. The blade was 23–30cm (9–12in) long, double-edged and slightly curved. Pistol-shaped grips were usually of jade or ivory, and the swords were often inlaid with gold and coloured stones.

KHANJARLI

The distinctive blade of the khanjarli has a re-curved look – it sweeps upwards and then appears to straighten out. The blade was 13–25cm (5–10in) long, and it came with or without knuckleguards. The hilts were usually ivory, and the pommel was fan shaped.

PATA

An exclusively Hindu weapon, the pata had a long, straight, usually double-edged blade, and it became popular at the time that European traders were establishing themselves in india. The blades were, therefore, usually made in Italy or Spain. The pata was accompanied by a metal attachment that protected the arm holding the weapon, making it into a gauntlet sword, and although using patas was a difficult technique to master, skilled pata swordsmen were among the best the subcontinent ever produced.

TALWAR

Perhaps the most respected of Indian edged weapons was the talwar, which is believed to have originated with the Mongols and to have been brought to India by the Moguls during the 16th century. The blade was deeply curved and tapered continuously to the tip, and was decorated with floral designs and personal inscriptions. The scabbard, which was usually of wood, was suspended from the belt by rings.

RIGHT:
Early 19th-century Indian Moghul dagger (khanjar) with carved jade hilt enamelled to resemble precious stones.

ABOVE:
19th-century Indian sword (talwar), its hilt damascened with gold.

LEFT AND BELOW:
Jade-hilted Indian sword (talwar), richly set with gold, rubies, emeralds and diamonds, damascened in gold on the blade with the name and badge (a tiger) of Tipu Sultan, 'Tiger of Mysore', killed in 1799 by British troops during the storming of his palace-fortress at Seringapathan.

RIGHT:
Mahratta (southern Indian) gauntlet sword or 'pata' from the 17th century. The blade is earlier (16th century) and imported from Europe.

INDONESIA

The area we know now as Indonesia – the islands of Sumatra, Java, Madura, the Lesser Sundas, the Moluccas, Celebes, about 3,000 smaller islands, together with the southern part of Borneo, the western part of New Guinea and East Timor – was an area of considerable military activity. The first great military power was the kingdom of Srividjaya in southern Sumatra, which existed in the 5th century. Thereafter, various powers came and went, until the area was so fractionalized that it fell easy prey to the colonial ambitions of the European powers, especially the Dutch. Despite its fragmented history, however, the area has produced some notable eged weapons.

KRIS

The kris is undoubtedly one of the best known and most effective of weapons. It is also sometimes called the Malay dagger. The kris is believed to have been originated in the 14th century by the king of Janggolo (a Moslem sultanate in central Java), but its history is shrouded in myth – indeed, local tradition avers that a good kris has a soul of its own.

The shape of the blade varied widely; in Java alone blades ranging from the almost straight to those undulating like a rapidly moving snake have been found. However, whatever the shape, the blade was formed from three layers of soft steel or iron, with thinner layers between. The blade was then beaten or twisted into shape. The blades of kris were usually double-edged and were 30–41cm (12–16in) long, although executioners' kris from Java were 60cm (24in) long. The kris was almost invariably decorated with engravings depicting dragons and demons. A ring, known as an uwar, fitted between the blade and the hilt, and this formed a primitive handguard as well as providing additional decoration and a means of suspending the weapon from a belt. Kris were usually kept in elaborately decorated scabbards embossed with brass or tortoiseshell motifs or painted figures.

Today, collectors should find few problems in beginning a collection of kris. They are still made in many parts of South-east Asia, and they are generally reasonably priced.

RIGHT:
Magnificent late 17th-century Malayan kris, the hilt of carved ivory depicting the god Vishnu, the scabbard overlaid with intricately-worked gold, the gold chape and hilt socket further enriched with cabochon rubies.

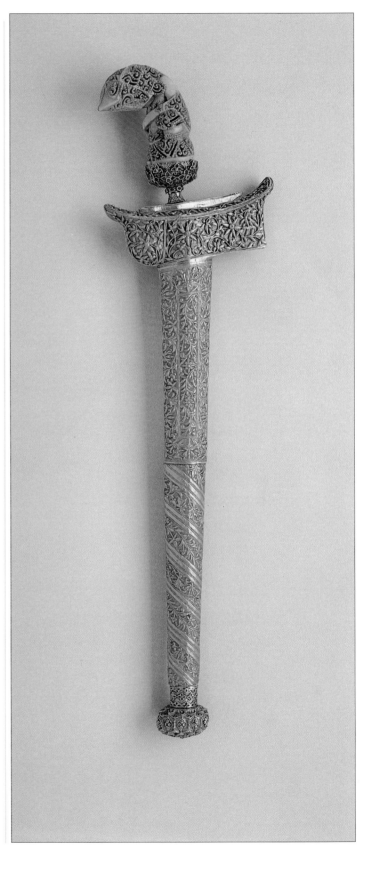

WEDONG

One of the most fascinating weapons to come from this area is the wedong, which resembled an elongated butcher's cleaver with sweeping lines along the cutting edge. Gold decorations were often added, while the sheaths were usually wood, lacquered red. The wedong was primarily a chopping weapon, and it is not impossible to acquire examples today, although antique ones are more difficult to find.

MANDAU

An interesting, all-purpose blade, the mandau is used by some of the tribes of Borneo, including the Dyaks. The word means 'head hunter', and it has been used for that purpose for centuries. The blade is usually single-edged, up to 50cm (20in) long and slightly curved. Handguards are rare, but the pommels are carved to represent ornate masks or figures. The mandau is unique in terms of edged weapons, and probably the only way to acquire one would be through a dealer with contacts in the area. It would be impossible to estimate the possible price or the history associated with any individual weapon.

ABOVE:
19th-century Java kris entirely overlaid with embossed and chased sheet silver.

RIGHT:
Silver mounted knife (golok) from the Malay peninsula; probably Javanese, mid-19th century.

RIGHT
Fabled Shogun Ieyasu at
Sekigahara (Barrier Field).
Waged in 1600, this crucial
battle foreshadowed the
Edo period, which made
Tokyo predominant in
Imperial affairs.

JAPAN

Until about the 5th century AD Japanese history remains shrouded in mystery, although the nation probably arose from the fusion of two peoples, those from Malaya or Polynesia and those from Asia, who conquered the Ainu, the original inhabitants. Jimmu Tenno, the leader of the Asiatic invaders, long regarded as a folk hero, has recently been accorded official status as Japan's first ruler. In the 5th century the art of writing was introduced from Korea, and in the 6th century Chinese culture became generally accepted, although attempts in the 7th century to establish a strong, centralized, Chinese-style monarchy to limit the power of the nobles failed. Real power was retained in the hands of the great feudal families, the daimyos (sometimes spelled daimios), until recent times.

In the 12th century a feudal military caste known as the samurai assumed power. The word, which means guard, was originally applied to all who bore arms, but eventually its use was restricted to the warrior knights and administrators who became retainers of the daimyos. The samurai remained in power until the fall of Tokugawa shogunate in 1867. They obeyed the bushido code (the way of the warrior) of bravery, honour and service. The code was a mixture of religious beliefs, social obligations and civic consciousness, and its basic tenet was that a worthy warrior lived constantly in such a way that he would be ready to die without warning with unsullied honour and memory.

In 1192 the ruling noble Yoritomo assumed the title shogun (commander in chief), a title that was borne until 1867 by the real ruler of Japan. During the 15th and 16th centuries Japan sank into a state of feudal anarchy, from which it was rescued between 1570 and 1615 by three great shoguns – Nobunaga, Hideyoshi and Ieyasu – and it was the family of the last of these, the Tokugawa, which continued to wield power until the emperor Meiji reasserted the power of the throne in 1867 and abolished the shogunate. During the next 30 years, the privileges of the nobility were abolished, a uniform code of law introduced and a constitution established.

The cult of the samurai has continued to exert a fascination: as recently as 1970 the Japanese author Yukio Mishima committed hara-kiri in protest at what he believed was the weakness of postwar Japan. The samurai's code was based on the veneration of the sword. Weapons were called nippon-to (soul of the samurai), and sword-makers were held in high esteem. Today, Japan has designated as official 'national treasures' 77 individuals who excel in traditional crafts; the number includes several weapon makers. Nippon-to are divided into four categories: the first, ka-to, includes real antiques of great intrinsic and extrinsic value; the second, shin-t́, includes those weapons made between 1700 and 1877 (the year of the Satsuma rebellion); the third group, shinshin-to, are those made between 1877 and World War II; and the fourth group, gun-to, includes the mass-produced weapons issued to officers and non-commissioned personnel during World War II.

What follows are descriptions of some of the better known edged weapons from Japan. Some of the smaller weapons appear at auction and through dealers from time to time, but aspiring collectors should be aware that the chances of legally acquiring examples of swords, except gun-to, are remote.

DAISHO

The daisho is not, in fact, one weapon, but two, and they were principal arms of the samurai. The main weapon was the long sword, the katana, while the second, originally known as the tanto, was the wakizashi.

The blade of a katana was 63–82cm (25–32in) long, although some of those made before 1700 were shorter. The wakizashi was shorter, although not by a great deal: the average length was 38–45cm (15–18in).

Daisho were laboriously made. The blades were formed of a soft iron alloyed with several prescribed grades of steel. During the manufacture, most of the blade was covered in a special paste of clay, sand and charcoal, leaving exposed the cutting edge, the yakiba, which was subjected to repeated heating and hammering until the maker was satisfied with the strength of the edge.

Many sets of daisho, especially examples of the katana, can be found outside Japan, but they are getting harder and more expensive to acquire. The Japanese government has recently launched a campaign to buy back daisho, especially from US collectors, and it is also reluctant to allow them to be sold for export.

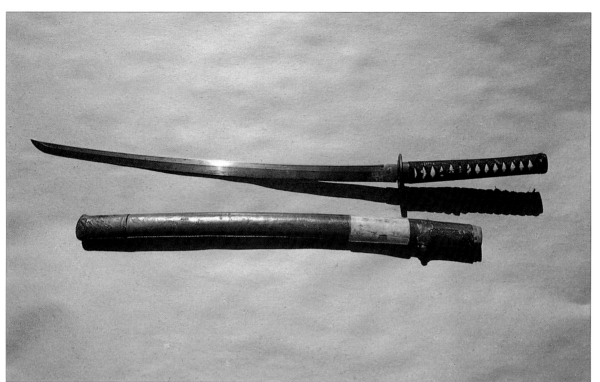

LEFT:
Historic samurai swords
outside Japan are quite
rare. This version of the
Katana, from a private US
collection, dates from
c 1700 and is apparently a
Shin-To.

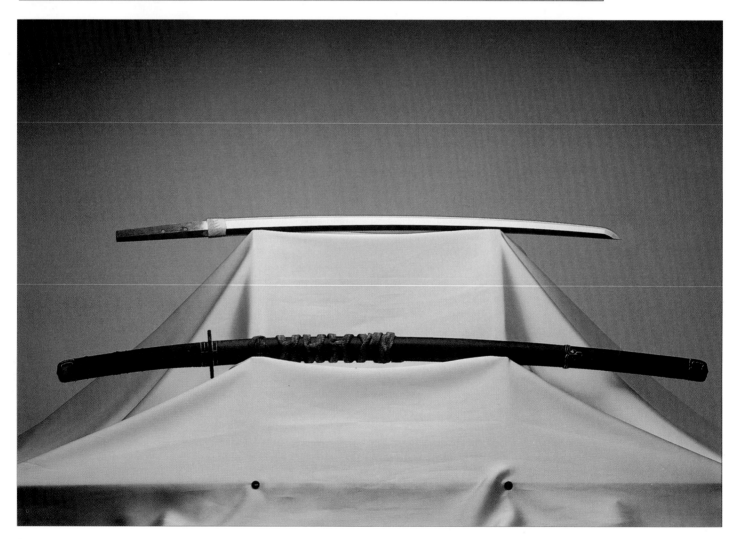

TOP:

Japanese dirk (wakizashi), 19th century. The by-knife (Kodzuka) is signed Sane Tsugu.

HAIKUCHI

Sometimes also known as aikuchi, the haikuchi is one of the best known of the plethora of shorter blades that were used in Japan. The name can be translated as 'pleasant companion', but they were, in fact, singularly nasty weapons. The hilt was usually wood with horn fittings, while the blades were 20–25cm (8–10in) long. They became popular in the 19th century, and were carried by people from all walks of life.

HAMIDASHI

The Japanese equivalent of the dirk, the hamidashi was an impressive weapon. It had a single-edged, slight curved blade, some 20–30cm (8–12in) long, and the hilt was usually bound with plaited cords over a covering of fish skin. For centuries the hamidashi enjoyed a reputation as the assassin's favoured weapon.

LEFT:

Japanese sword (katana) of the early 19th century; the blade, however, dates from the late 15th century, and was made by the Mihara school of swordsmiths in the Bingo Province of south-west Japan.

KWAIKEN

This interesting blade was an old-fashioned dagger designed for women. It could be used defensively, having a double-edged blade, some 20–30cm (8–12in) long, and a plain scabbard of lacquered wood, but it was also meant to be used for seppuku, ritual suicide by hara-kiri, if a woman faced disgrace.

NAGAMAKI

A two-handed weapon, somewhat akin to a halberd, the nagamaki could be attached to a shorter handle and used as a sword. It became popular in about 1600 and continued to be widely used, even during the restructuring of Japanese society that began in 1867. Soldiers called upon to use it had to be especially trained. A few nagamaki are thought to be in collections outside Japan, but they are unlikely to become available for sale.

NO-DACHI

One of the weapons seen in Japanese art, the no-dachi is the field sword. These enormous weapons, with blades often as long as 2m (6ft), were carried across the back. Special echelons of soldiers were trained to use it in spearhead attacks to break open enemy lines, but it never achieved widespread acceptance. The no-dachi was strictly a fighting weapon, and the scabbards were made of plain wood and bore little decoration. Few no-dachi were made, and the chances of acquiring one are remote.

TACHI

The tachi is, perhaps, the most historic of all Japanese edged weapons. It was the original sword of the samurai. The blades were usually 60–70cm (24–28in) long, although some later examples were 50–60cm (20–24in) long. The tachi was hung, edge downwards from the belt by two straps. The scabbard was made of wood overlaid with metal, and both sword hilt and scabbard were decorated with floral and mythical motifs. Although the daisho replaced it as the preferred weapon of the samurai, the tachi remained the weapon that was worn at court and on ceremonial occasions, and when it was not in use, it was carefully protected and stored away.

The chances of a collector specializing in Oriental weaponry being able legally to acquire a tachi today are virtually nil.

KHUKRI

The khukri or kukri is the knife carried by the Gurkhas. It has a forward-angled blade with a pistol-grip hilt. The blade is heavy, single-edged and weighted towards the point, allowing a blow of maximum impact to be delivered with minimum effort. The straight hilt is usually made of wood or ivory, there is no handguard, and the pommel is disc shaped. Smaller blades are also sometimes carried in sheath, although the khukri itself was used for chopping almost anything from necks to firewood.

During World War II many Allied soldiers were perplexed by a curious scene. A Gurkha would always let anyone look at the blade of his khukri, but, before returing it to its sheath, he would always prick his finger with it. This was done because tradition said that a weapon could

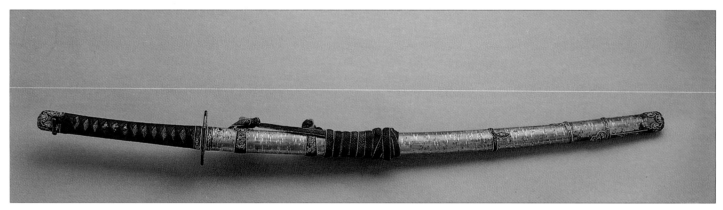

NEPAL

This independent country in the Himalayas has produced some of the greatest warriors of recent times. The country developed as a group of feudal kingdoms, and although the Gurkhas conquered the kingdoms and established modern Nepal in 1769, the individual leaders of the subject kingdoms tended to show more loyalty to their own clans than to the nation. The history of the 18th and 19th centuries is one of assassination and palace intrigue, and from 1846 the king was nothing more than a figurehead. In 1815–16 Nepal was, after a prolonged and bloody struggle, subjugated by Britain and the Gurkhas were recruited into the British Army, in which, until recently, as many as 80,000 of these fearless fighters continued to serve.

not be returned to its sheath by a living Gurkha without tasting blood.

KORA

The national sword of Nepal is actually the kora, which dates from the 9th century. The distinctive blade, which is approximately 60cm (2ft) long, curves inward, and there are concave incisions in the tip. Near the lower one is always found the Buddhist symbol of a lotus flower surrounded by a circle. Nowadays, the hilt is usually made of steel, although it is possible to find older examples with brass hilts. The grip is tubular and is held between two disc-shaped objects. Scabbards are fashioned in leather and decorated with embroidered velvet.

ABOVE:
Late 18th-century Japanese sword (tachi)

OVERLEAF:
The 'Holbein' dagger is so called because of the Dance of Death design on many of the sheaths. This is directly based on a drawing by that artist for a dagger-sheath in the Basel Museum. These are all mid 16th-century Swiss examples, displaying subtle variations.

CHAPTER FIVE

COLLECTING
AND CARING
FOR YOUR
ACQUISITIONS

COLLECTING AND CARING FOR YOUR ACQUISITIONS

HOW TO COLLECT

It might be thought that only recent weapons can be collected in the traditional sense. It is, of course, true that the older the weapon, the more it will cost and the harder and longer will be the struggle to obtain it. But they can be acquired. Private and aristocratic collections are dispersed from time to time, and interesting and unusual items are constantly appearing on the market. For example, an auction at Sotheby's, London, in 1990 included among the lots an extremely rare Lloyd's Patriotic Fund presentation sword, an early 15th-century Italian weapon and a British cavalry sabre that may have been used at Waterloo. Sotheby's is not the only auction house in the UK, much less the only one in the world.

Before you spend any money at all, visit as many museums and exhibitions of militaria and edged weapons as you can. Some of the major collections of edged weapons are listed on page xxx, but many museums include displays of edged weapons, and you should never pass up the opportunity to look at as many different kinds as you can. You will probably meet people who share your own enthusiasm, and you may even meet dealers and begin to develop contacts.

You should also read as much as you can on the subject. As well as having books on the subject, your local library should also be able to supply you with the names and addresses of local and national organizations. Many of these publish journals and newsletters, and it is well worth getting on their mailing lists. The US publisher, House of Collectibles, 1900 Premier Row, Orlando Central Park, Orlando, Florida, USA 32809, produces a large number of books on all aspects of collecting, including knives and other edged weapons. Most publications deal with weapons made after 1500, but, unless you are determined to acquire especially antique weapons, this is, in any case, most likely to be your period of interest.

It is also important to make contact with dealers and auction houses. Most of these are reputable – indeed, dishonest dealers quickly go out of business. Get on mailing lists so that you receive advance information about forthcoming specialist sales. It is also worth while telling dealers if you have a particular area of interest or are trying to acquire an example of a particular type of weapon.

COST

Collecting can be expensive. Even the cheapest historic or moderately rare weapon is not something you are likely to acquire by tossing down your credit card. It is, of course, an insoluble problem. Some people feel they have been cheated if they pay a certain amount for an object and find, a year later, that they could obtain it elsewhere for less. This is nonsense. The prices of collectables are determined by the laws of supply and demand: what a particular weapon is worth depends on what the seller can get for it and what the buyer will give at any particular time.

LOOKING AFTER YOUR COLLECTION

Sadly, one of the first problems that you will have to consider is security. It is wise never to make the contents of your collection well known to anyone who is not completely trustworthy and do not arrange your collection on a wall that can be seen by passers-by. It is also worth installing some form of home security system.

You must insure your collection. All your weapons should be photographed, in colour if possible and from several angles, and any distinguishing marks should be photographed and listed separately. It is impossible to suggest what sort of premiums you will have to pay, although they are likely to be high. Nevertheless, insuring your collection is vital.

The very nature of weapons means that they are far more durable than, say, glass or porcelain. However, the greatest enemy of all metal weapons is moisture, which will cause rust. Protect your collection by keeping your weapons sheathed at all times and, if possible, by storing them under glass. Rust often starts to attack metal in small scratches and nicks. Begin with the blade, and polish it carefully with a fine abrasive; then protect it with Vaseline or oil.

Keep your weapons away from direct sunlight. The infrared rays will cause any non-metallic parts – wood, bone or ivory handles, for instance – to fade, and this will detract from the appearance and thus the value of the item.

If for some reason you have to transport any of your collection you should take a number of precautions. First, do not tell anyone what you are proposing to do. Then, you must take care to ensure that your weapons are not damaged in transit. Some collectors, working on the theory that it was what cutlery salesmen used to do, advocate wrapping blades in oilcloth. There is also a specially treated type of leather cloth available; do *not* use ordinary leather, which contains tanning acids that can not only increase rusting but even generate corrosion.

FAKES AND FORGERIES

Fortunately, so far at least, militaria does not seem to have attracted the fakers and forgers that have bedevilled many other areas of collectables. One of the main ways of avoiding mistakes, however, is to know as much as possible about the subject – then there can be no danger of buying a Roman 'long sword'.

A story that may well be apocryphal illustrates the point. A wealthy Japanese investor was visiting the US when he was accosted by a man who looked down and out. The man wanted to sell a short sword of some kind to the visitor; he was destitute and willing to let it go for as little as $25,000 even though it was such an important weapon – the blade with which Japanese war leader and prime minister Hideki Tojo had committed hara-kiri at the end of World War II. The patriotic Japanese businessman 'salvaged' the sword as a matter of national pride. When he returned home he learnt that Hideki Tojo had shot himself.

It is your responsibility as a collector to know as much as possible about the period in which you are interested. You will pick up a lot of general knowledge as you visit exhibitions and talk to other collectors, but that will not be enough. You should study the period in detail.

Before you buy you should always examine the weapon carefully. Do all the parts seem to belong

RIGHT:
A 19th-century copy of a Renaissance sword (perhaps based on the sword of Philip the Fair in Vienna); the blade, however, is an original Italian one, *c* 1500.

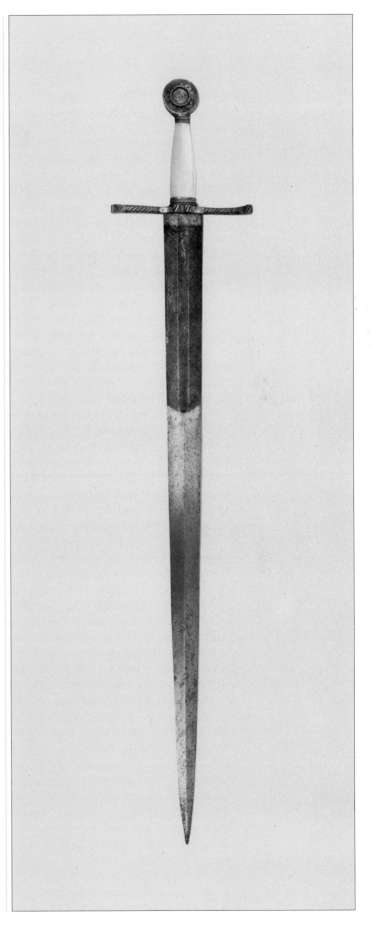

together? Are the blade, hilt and crossguard compatible and well placed? Does the handle look artificially aged and as if it had been 'married' to an older blade? Are the hilt and grip in exquisite condition while the blade is chipped and scratched?

Look especially at old engravings of the maker's mark or signature. If you are considering purchasing an Oriental weapon and you find on it a reference to, say, the 1877 Satsuma Rebellion, it is clearly not a ka-to samurai sword dating from before 1700.

Try to see if the marks have been properly put on. If they were lightly stamped or badly adhered, they can easily be excised with a sharp knife tip. As a general rule – although nothing is invariable – identifying marks, swordmakers' signatures, Oriental 'chops' and so forth were put on the blade or tang before the weapon received its final heat treatment. They should not come off.

The blades of smaller weapons can be flexed. An old, brittle blade, attached to a weapon that is purportedly fairly new, may even splinter. In addition, the blade may not be properly seated within its new handle. The tang might not be properly formed to fit snugly inside – if it rattles, forget it. There is, however, no foolproof way of testing a blade yourself – and even experts fail on occasions.

Never buy anything you are not sure about. Of course, everyone makes mistakes, but you can protect yourself from some basic errors. The scimitar, for example, was originally considered to be solely a combat weapon. There should normally be nothing but the name of the maker or owner or a brief religious text engraved on it. If someone tries to sell you a lavishly ornamented 'scimitar' keep your wallet in your pocket.

One of the best ways to avoid problems of this kind is to buy through dealers, brokers and auction houses, all of which are or employ experts in the various fields in which you may be interested. These professionals guard their reputations jealously, and it is certainly not in their interests for a client to think he has been duped.

Always beware the great 'bargain'. You may meet someone who has, say, a 19th-century Bowie knife that he is prepared 'to let go' cheaply because he is down on his luck. Move away very quickly. Why on earth should a stranger want to do you a favour? If times are really that hard, why is he trying to sell an object worth several hun-

dred, maybe thousands of pounds, for a fraction of its value? But people are taken in by people like this. Use your common sense and avoid falling into traps of this kind.

Finally, a word about restorations. Some people believe that if a weapon is not precisely the way it was made, it is not authentic. This is not the case: weapons are like cars, and they can be repaired as long as *authentic* parts are used in the repair. However, repair and restoration should always be left to experts. Never try to straighten weakened metal and never, never glue pieces together. A badly repaired or restored item may be worth less than the damaged article.

MUSEUMS TO VISIT

Almost every country has at least one museum or institution where a major collection of edged weapons may be seen. Those listed below are those whose collections are generally regarded as wide ranging and historically complete.

Austria
Historisches Museum der Stadt Wien, Vienna
Landeszenghaus, Graz
Waffensammlung, Vienna

Belgium
Porte de Hal, Brussels

Czechoslovakia
Castle Collaredo-Mansfield, Opocno

Denmark
Tojhusmet, Copenhagen

France
Musée de l'Armée, Paris
Musée du Louvre, Paris
Musée Massena Joubert Collection, Nice

Germany
Historisches Museum, Dresden
Museum für Deutsche Geschichte, Berlin

Italy
Museo Nazionale, Florence
Museum Stibbert Collection, Florence

Netherlands
Rijksmuseum voor Volkenkunde, Leiden

Poland
Wawel Armoury, Cracow

Spain
Armoury, Palacio Réal de Madrid, Madrid

Sweden
Kungl Livrustkammaren, Stockholm

Switzerland
Landesmuseum, Zurich
Historischemuseum, Basle

UK
The Armouries, Tower of London, London
Castle Museum, York
Fitzwilliam Museum, Cambridge
Imperial War Museum, London
Museum of London, Barbican Centre, London
Royal Scottish Museum, Edinburgh
Wallace Collection, Manchester Square, London
Windsor Castle Museum, Windsor
Victoria & Albert Museum, London

USA
Allentown Art Museum, Pennsylvania
Brooklyn Museum, New York
Chicago Museum of History, Illinois
City Art Museum, St Louis, Missouri
Cleveland Museum of Art, Ohio
Metropolitan Museum of Art, New York
National Knife Museum, Chattanooga, Tennessee
Smithsonian Institution, Washington DC
West Point Museum, West Point, New York

USSR
State Hermitage Museum, Leningrad

BIBLIOGRAPHY

Dozens of books on various aspects of collecting edged weapons are available, but, as this book has concentrated on both the history of edged weapons as well as the opportunities to collect them, this bibliography is restricted to similar works that deal with the historical background to a limited number or type of weaponry. Sadly, most of the books listed here are now out of print and are likely to be available only through libraries.

Abels, Robert, *Classic Bowie Knives,* 1967

Annis, P.G.W., *Naval Swords,* Stackpole Books, Harrisburg, PA, 1970

Childe, V.G., *The Bronze Age,* Cambridge University Press, 1930

Cornish, F.W., *Chivalry,* privately published, London, 1911

Cowper, H.S., *The Art of Attack and Development of Weapons,* privately published, 1906

Dean, Bashford, *Japanese Armor,* Metropolitan Museum of Art, New York, 1903

Dean, Bashford, *Catalogue of European Arms and Armor,* Metropolitan Museum of Art, New York, 1905

Denison, Lt Col G.T., *A History of Cavalry,* London, 1877

Grancsay, S.V., *Arms and Armor,* Allentown Art Museum, Pennsylvania, 1964

Gyngell, D.S.H., *Armorers' Marks,* Cambridge University Press, New York, 1963

Hutton, Capt Alfred, *The Sword and the Centuries,* 1901

Henderson, James, *Sword Collecting for Amateurs,* Frederick Muller, London, 1969

Mann, Sir James, *Catalogue of the Wallace Collection,* London, 1962

May, W.E., *Naval Swords and Firearms,* London, 1962

Neumann, G.C., *Swords and Blades of the American Revolution,* Stackpole Books, Harrisburg, PA, 1973

Nickel, Helmut, *Warriors and Worthies,* Atheneum Press, New York, 1969

Norman, A.V.B., *Small Swords and Military Swords,* London, 1967

Peterson, H.L., *The American Sword,* Walker Co, New York, 1975

Peterson, H.L., *Daggers and Fighting Knives of the Western World,* Walker Co., New York, 1968

Rogers, Col H.C.B., *Mounted Troops of the British Army,* London, 1959

Schobel, J., *Fine Arms and Armor,* Menton Books, New York, 1975

Stone, George C., *A Glossary of Arms and Armor,* Brussel Co., Boston, 1934

Tarassuk, L., *The Encyclopedia of Arms and Weapons,* Bonanza Books, New York, 1986

Thimm, C.A., *The Complete Bibliography of Fencing and Duelling,* privately published, London, 1896

Valentine, Eric, *Rapiers,* Stackpole Books, Harrisburg, PA, 1970

Wagner, Edward, *Cut and Thrust Weapons,* Spring Books, London, 1967

Wallace, John, *Scottish Swords and Dirks,* Stackpole Books, Harrisburg, PA, 1970

Wilkinson, Frederick, *Swords and Daggers,* Lock & Co., London, 1967

Wise, A., *The History and Art of Personal Combat,* New York, 1935

LEFT:
François Clouet, *Portrait
of Francis I*, c1545.

INDEX

PICTURE CREDITS